making it happen

making
presentations
happen

A simple and effective guide
to speaking with confidence and power

Michael Brown

ALLEN&UNWIN

First published in 2001 as *Media Easy* by Media Associates
This edition first published in 2003 by Allen & Unwin

Allen & Unwin
83 Alexander Street
Crows Nest NSW 2065
Australia
Phone: (61 2) 8425 0100
Fax: (61 2) 9906 2218
Email: info@allenandunwin.com
Web: www.allenandunwin.com

National Library of Australia
Cataloguing-in-Publication entry:

Brown, Michael, 1948–.
  Making presentations happen: a simple and effective guide
  for speaking with confidence and power.
  Bibliography.
  Includes index.
  ISBN 1 86508 958 3.

  1. Public speaking — Handbooks, manuals, etc. 2. Oral
  communication — Handbooks, manuals, etc. I. Title.
  (Series: Making it happen).
808.51

Layout by Coral Lee
Text design by Peta Nugent
Printed by South Wind Production, Singapore

10 9 8 7 6 5 4 3 2 1

about

the series

making it happen

Are you committed to changing things for the better? Are you searching for ways to make your organisation more effective? Are you trying to help your people and organisation to improve, but are seriously strapped for time and money? If you are, then this Making It Happen book is written specifically for you.

Every book in the series is designed to assist change agents to get things done ... to make new programs really happen ... without costing the organisation an arm and a leg and without taking up all of your valuable time.

Each book in the series is written by a top consultant in the field who does not simply theorise about their subject of expertise but who explains specifically how to implement a program that will really work for your work unit or organisation. Vital advice on what works and what doesn't work, what tricks to use and traps to avoid, plus suggested strategies for implementation, templates and material to photocopy, and checklists to gauge your readiness — each book in the series is filled with useful information, all written in clear, practical language that enables you to make things happen, fast.

Help your people and work unit to increase their performance and love their work through implementing a program from the Making It Happen series and reap the rewards that successful change agents deserve.

a b o u t

the book

Butterflies in your stomach? Cold, clammy hands? Dry, parched throat? Ask almost anyone to speak in front of an audience and these can be just some of the many symptoms which render a normally confident person nervous and a little shaky. Most of us will go out of our way to avoid speaking in public, and when we can't avoid it, we often wish we could be more prepared.

The philosophy behind *Making Presentations Happen* assumes that what you are in front of an audience is much more important than what you do. Why? Because an audience can see right through you — on a subconscious level at least. And (again subconsciously) we all know that; which explains why public speaking always goes to number one on our list of greatest fears.

This book provides you with the tools to present with confidence and authority. You will learn everything from selecting the right audiovisuals to handling tough questions from your audience. *Making Presentations Happen* shows you how to overcome nervousness and take control of your presentations so that your message is communicated clearly and effectively.

But reading about presenting in front of an audience is not enough in itself; you must practise in real-life situations. Included in this book are activities, checklists and tools for the active development of your presentation skills.

With the simple techniques in this book, you'll learn how to speak to your audiences with confidence and power, harnessing your nervous energy into a dynamic and effective presentation.

about
the author

Michael Brown began a career in television journalism in 1977. He was a reporter, director and presenter of various news and current affairs programs for Television New Zealand over the next 14 years. He has also worked on secondment for the BBC.

These days, Michael is a trainer and consultant in communication skills for Media Associates, based in New Zealand. His clients include government departments, SOEs, CRIs, DHBs and big business. His pleasure — and self-confessed obsession — is helping people overcome their fear to perform confidently in public.

Michael has also written the training book *Making Effective Media Happen: A simple and effective guide for dealing with the media*.

He has also published two novels: *The Weaver's Apprentice* and *The Idiot Played Rachmaninov*, plus two travel books: *The Weaver and the Abbey* and *The Taming of the Crew* (written after he and his family sold everything and sailed away into the worst storms for half a century).

He has a B.Sc. (Hons) degree in Physics, a Diploma in Teaching and a post-graduate Diploma in Journalism (Canterbury).

Michael can be reached at *michael.brown@media-associates.co.nz*

contents

chapter 1

Why learn to speak in public?

- The power of projecting fundamental respect

- Making nervousness work for you

- Programming the subconscious with visualisation

'I believe it would be a very good idea.'
Mahatma Gandhi, when asked what he thought of Western civilization

As we head into the twenty-first century, we see a new spirit emerging. The change is particularly marked in Western business. *Forbes* magazine says the sharks are learning how to succeed in business by being nice to their competitors. Herb Cohen's world best-seller *You Can Negotiate Anything* is dedicated to a man whose negotiating strategy was always to give much more than he received. Then there's Stephen Covey's immensely popular *Seven Habits of Highly Effective People* (1993). It says that in the long run you cannot succeed at using strategies to influence people if your character is fundamentally flawed. Not behaviour, not personality — character. And what about the Huthwaite Group's startling discoveries? In a study of 10 000 salespeople across 50 companies and 23 countries, the Huthwaite Group found a highly successful sales method based on the implication that genuine interest in the customer brings better sales. The same study found that for larger sales, many of the hallowed methods of manipulating people simply don't work in the long term and never have worked: these methods were only kept alive and pumping by anecdotal evidence.

The implications of the changing mind-set are staggering. It means that whatever techniques and strategies you use and whatever short-term gains you might make, people somehow *know*! Think of it. Consciously or subconsciously they sense what you are and are more strongly influenced by that than anything you *do*. The change also implies that mutual respect and cooperation bring better material rewards.

Astounding. But wait, haven't we heard that one somewhere before? Hasn't it been around for ... well ... at least two thousand years? Of course it has. It's just that the message only began to be recognised in the last decade by the hard-nosed business community. Believe it or not, twentieth century people-management systems and models grew from nineteenth century military models because — as presumed by industrialists — the military were the only organisations that knew how to get people to do what was necessary.

It's hard to imagine a paradigm shift more significant. The implications for leadership and the management of people are enormous. And so are the implications for the way we persuade, convince or inform people who gather in one place to listen to us.

What we are internally has a profound, subconscious impact on our audiences.

In an old Wayne and Schuster skit, Dr Tex Rorschach (*Have Couch Will Travel*) interviews a patient lying on a saloon bar.

Patient: You mean if I like them, they're going to like me?

Dr Rorschach: Siggie Freud couldn't have put it better.

My most significant interview in 15 years of broadcasting taught me the same point. I was talking to a dying five-year-old girl. Nicola had terminal muscular atrophy. She was still well enough to be at school, although in a wheelchair. She was extraordinarily popular with her classmates, winning their respect and attention far beyond any sense of pity or duty. In the middle of the interview I commented on that popularity. Recognising it for the question it was, she screwed up her face to think about it.

'I think it's because I like them,' she said.

That, from a five-year-old! It's not the kind of inner quality that can be switched on and off in front of an audience. It is the kind of quality that can only be encouraged to rise from deep within.

We can take this much further. Liking — of others or ourselves — is just part of an even more significant concept for presenters: inner strength and personal power.

■ PERSONAL POWER

Audiences are irresistibly attracted to and impressed by personal power. Countless audiences — without consciously knowing it — are more swayed by a presenter's personal power than by their facts or logic.

For excellent presenters in the making, it's useful to pull personal power into two categories. The first is *connected* personal power: the power to connect with your audience. Notice that this is power 'with' not power 'over'. Also, don't think for one moment that I'm suggesting sainthood as a prerequisite. That's because the second type of personal power exists quite apart from any system of ethics: it's *separate* personal power — the inner strength that stands alone without depending on or being affected by others.

FIGURE 1.1
Connected personal power versus separate personal power

Great presenters with
connected personal power
give us the feeling that they:

- know my strengths and weaknesses and are comfortable with them

- believe in my inner strength

- respect me

- want me to feel passionate about their topic yet respect my right and ability to make up my own mind

- want to be here talking to me.

Great presenters with
separate personal power
give us the feeling that they:

- know their own strengths and weaknesses and are comfortable with them

- believe in their own inner strength

- respect themselves

- feel passionately about their topic and know their own minds

- want to be where they are right now.

Of course, great presenters don't say any of that in words. They don't need to. They've simply chosen to adopt those attitudes and we can sense it.

We can all think of hugely influential speakers — John F. Kennedy, Winston Churchill, Martin Luther King, Adolf Hitler — but that could be a distraction because it's too easy to make their abilities unreachable with words like *charisma*, or the *'X' factor*, as if they were caused by some mysterious quality you need to be born with. You don't. Winston Churchill certainly wasn't: he suffered from speaker's nerves even more than most (see page 10).

Both types of personal power are inherent in all of us, usually masked by our pasts and our beliefs.

I know from my workshops that most people don't want to become brilliant, ball-of-fire orators. They just want to be good enough to be good. Good enough to look confident, credible and authoritative. I want to convince you that you can achieve that and, if you want, much much more.

How do we get this personal power? The rest of this book is the answer to that question.

■ GETTING POWER BY GIVING RESPECT

Shakespeare neatly exposed the underlying connection between us all:

'All the world's a stage, and all the men and women merely players.'

Many of us forget that we are actors bound by mutual agreement. But those who command widespread respect and are considered wise are usually those who feel that connection and who then allow it to show in their manner. I call that feeling 'fundamental respect': the respect you feel for every individual, regardless of circumstance, *because they breathe the same air as you do*. It's quiet. It's subtle. You don't wear it on your sleeve, you don't hit your audiences over the head with it, but it is a practical way to apply what Nicola did. It's a practical way to begin building your personal power.

That may seem strange when Mick Jones back there in the fourth row keeps interjecting aggressively and is known to mug old ladies and take rusks from the mouths of babies. I'm not suggesting you have to like him. Fundamental respect has little to do with everyday 'like' and 'dislike', 'agree' and 'disagree', 'with us' and 'against us'.

Fundamental respect does not change with circumstance or the wind.

It's very, *very* subtle. Yet those who cultivate fundamental respect for others cannot help but emanate strength and presence. There is nothing wimpish about fundamental respect — you can *fire* someone while practising it and, in spite of the pain inflicted, that person will respect you.

■ FEEL YOUR WAY

'Feelings are the great generator of the universe.' Douglas Adams, *The Hitch Hiker's Guide to the Galaxy*

René Descartes got it wrong. His famous line, 'I think, therefore I am', should have been 'I feel, therefore I am'.

Recent research on the brain backs that up. Consider this: in the brain the neocortex is associated with decisions based on thinking, planning and problem solving. Beneath the neocortex is the mid-brain, which cannot read, write or think, and yet it feels emotions and is often called the 'feeling' brain. Are you one who says, 'I pride myself on making logical decisions'? Here's the bad news. In 1996, Iowa neurosurgeon Antonio Damasio showed — in one of the previous decade's most significant discoveries — that the neocortex does not make decisions until it has 'checked out' the mid-brain. In other words, emotions are central to process of rational thought. Your feelings are central to most of your decisions. The things that transform us are feelings, not logic.

The implication for an audience is obvious. And it means a lot for people learning how to be better presenters.

> **We may agree that a communication principle is right or intellectually correct, but it will only improve our skills when we register a feeling or attitude about it.**

I've designed many of the activities so that you can, if you choose, deliberately involve your feelings and attitudes. In this case, it's a matter of 'first with the heart, then with the head'.

Let me go a little further and apply the idea to the audience. When we speak to an audience — no matter how learned or rational they are — we are speaking largely to heart, not head. To our instincts.

■ WHICH PART OF A SPEECH CARRIES THE GREATEST IMPACT?

We can quantify this, working on two assumptions: that facts are rarely perceived as emotionally neutral and that feelings and attitudes are important to conveying any message containing facts.

Working on these assumptions, in 1967 psychologist Albert Mehrabian analysed the way a speaker's attitudes and feelings impact on an audience. He asked what proportion of the perceived attitudes/feelings are in the verbal content (the meaning of the words)? How much is in the vocal content (tones)? How much is in the visual content (body language)? As shown in Figure 1.2, the results were startling.

FIGURE 1.2

The impact of a speaker's feelings and attitudes on an audience

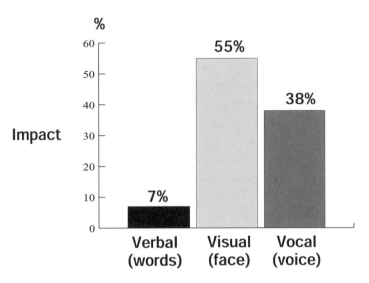

Mehrabian himself questioned the assumptions behind the experiment, but he also said it was likely to have a broader applicability. I'm going to assume that we can apply the results to a general situation.

If we combine the last two columns, we get what we see in Figure 1.3.

FIGURE 1.3

Your words versus how you present them

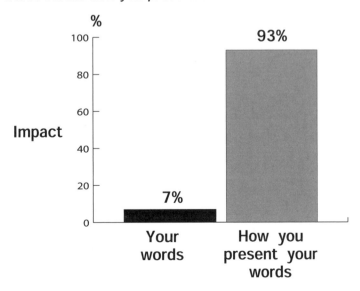

The conclusion is inescapable:

> **Your ability to persuade or convince depends very little on what you say and almost entirely on how you say it.**

Some find that extraordinary, some find it sobering. And yet everything in my acting, broadcasting and public speaking experience supports it. Of the speakers you listen to, how much content do you recall five minutes later? Or do you remember the feelings and attitudes of the speaker? Do you remember the seller's proposal, or the feelings you had about the seller and the proposal? Almost always in the memory stakes, the intellectual content comes in a poor second.

One reservation: if your audience has a particular interest in your message, it will be particularly tuned into content. For example, your own staff, colleagues and bosses. For those, I believe the figure of seven per cent is too low, sometimes much too low.

Even so, there's no escaping the fact that our word content — of its own accord — does very little to persuade or convince our audiences! Some of the managers and executives in my workshops react by declaring pessimistically that it almost doesn't matter what you say. Of course that's going too far; we simply can't replace content with manner and style.

Even so, we've arrived at this point:

> ***You* are the medium. *You* are most of your message.**

I hope that's sobering to those who have grafted onto themselves comforting jargon, safe officialese, grand phrases, pre-written and monotonal speeches. Each is capable of turning your speech into a stone that slips into a pond casting no ripples. Within seconds there's no sign that it ever happened. The blank faces in the audience mask a desire for it to end and the polite applause is relief that it did. When that happens you can forget informing or entertaining your audiences and you can forget persuading and convincing them to do or think anything.

Are you shocked by the implications for your presentations? Who can blame you if you believed that the job of a presenter is simply to present the facts? Now you know it isn't.

> **Good presenters do not dispense information, they translate it.**

When we drop our knowledge and expertise on an audience and see blank, puzzled faces, guess whose fault it is? It's ours. Ours because we did not translate our language into the language of this particular audience.

Some scientists protest. 'The facts are the facts', they say. 'Two plus two equals four, regardless of the audience.' But that's not the point. It's not a presenter's job to give the information that two plus two equals four; rather to give an *understanding* that two plus two equals four. That's a huge difference. And for scientists, think of this: being objective does not mean dispensing every fact. You can translate, select, reject, highlight, illustrate, emphasise, summarise and paraphrase to suit the perceptions of the audience — and still remain impartial. Einstein understood that. He said, 'If you can't explain it to a six-year-old, you don't understand it yourself.'

■ MAKING NERVOUSNESS WORK FOR YOU

'And Moses said, "Please, Lord, don't send me. I was never a good speaker and I haven't become one since you began speaking to me."' Free translation of Exodus 4:10

Moses was so terrified of speaking in front of others that, even under the glowering brow of the Lord, he dug his toes into the sand and refused. The Almighty, not having foreseen this eventuality, was irritated. But confronted by fear even more awesome than His wrath, even He conceded defeat, put a hold on the bolt of lightning, and summoned Moses' brother Aaron to do the spokesman job.

Fear of public speaking — media interviews and live presentations — is not like other fears. At rest, the human heart beats about 70 times per minute. While we are waiting to speak it can go as high as 190 beats per minute. That would lead to cardiac arrest if it was sustained, but after 30 seconds or so, it does head down. There's only one other kind of stress reputed to have the same effect. Fear of death. In one study of 3000 people in the US, the number of people who chose public speaking as their greatest fear exceeded the number who chose flying and the number who chose death *added together*. Which seems to mean that many would rather drop dead at 35 000 feet than speak in public.

Why so deeply fearful? We all know, intuitively, that an audience is the most efficient x-ray machine in the world. We know that the moment we open our mouths in front of an audience, all our protective veils will be instantly transparent. We know that the amount of inner personal power we believe we have *is going to be totally exposed*. One standard nightmare has many of us walking out on stage only to discover that we're dressed for our original birthday. The reaction of an audience to a speaker hamstrung by nerves is devastating; first pity, then contempt. Is it any wonder we feel anxiety, or outright fear?

We must find an answer.

You might have tried will power. You might have tried logic, lecturing yourself in ringing tones like this: 'Fear is itself the biggest obstacle. Therefore it would be irrational to allow it to affect me. Therefore fear is no longer an option.' Tried it? Doesn't work too well, does it? The nervous plumbing adjustment is still required. That's because conscious opposition of fear doesn't even begin to cope with the subconscious forces involved. It's like trying to set the dogs on a deepwater shark. Even a mild case of nerves cannot be overcome by willing it to stop, because conscious willpower and fear of public speaking simply will not climb into the same boxing ring.

So, opposing the fear directly is *not* the answer.

Consider this. When you know that the true extent of your personal power is going to be exposed, your subconscious senses DANGER! Each of us is a bus, carrying a load of ancestors. You have a contract with them in which they agree to keep quiet most of the time, but when a collision looms they're allowed to get into the driver's seat with you.

You wouldn't kick them out; it's a very sensible contract. Your ancestors learnt how to avoid becoming lion's lunch. They developed surges of adrenaline that allowed for very fast, top-performing reactions. That's why you're alive now. That's why you experience signs of danger-readiness like a dry mouth, wet armpits, cold sweaty palms, swallowing, increased heart rate and blood pressure. Sound familiar?

You can see where I'm heading. This kind of fear is not an enemy, it's a friend — waiting to be recognised and to help you survive. You conquer this kind of fear by using it as your ancestors did: *as a necessary tool for top performance.*

Put your fear into gear. Use your nervous energy to make sure you fire on all cylinders.

See if you can pick this character: as a schoolboy he was shy and awkward in front of his classmates. He went on to distinguish himself in the Boer War and became an MP in the House of Commons. Even so, he was still so fearful of public speaking that in the middle of one of his addresses, he lisped, stuttered and collapsed in a heap on the floor. That was Winston Churchill, who went on to become better admired as a speaker than as a prime minister.

So you don't have to be a natural. Most speakers are not born, they're self-made. Your current performance has nothing to do with your potential, which is unlimited. Unless you believe otherwise, of course. Henry Ford said it: 'Whether you think you can or whether you think you can't, you are probably right.'

■ LEADERSHIP

This book is not about another management skill. It's about the verbal, vocal and body language of leadership. When major companies hire a top executive, what attribute do you think is at the very top of their priority list? Ability to organise? Ability to draft good policy? Ability to see clearly to the horizon and plot a course? Certainly they're important, but right at the top is something else: the ability to persuade, convince and inspire the people who run the ship so that it sails smoothly on.

Speak well in front of others and you are noted, consciously or subconsciously by your audiences, as someone who is destined for higher things. For the ambitious, learning to speak in public is the fastest and most direct track to respect, admiration and promotion. For those who simply want to survive the experience, learning to speak in public is also a fast-track to improving self-esteem. And the amazing thing is that it's not difficult. You'll find the steps simple to understand and follow. However, there may be a catch. Are you determined to be good at this?

- How willing are you to practise what you read? Speaking in public is one skill you can't get simply by reading!
- How strongly can you picture yourself speaking well in public? Close your eyes ... do you see an appreciative audience, or do you see boredom?

■ VISUALISATION: THE SUBCONSCIOUS PROGRAMMING THAT WORKS

'Imagination rules the world.' Napoleon Bonaparte

Our beliefs have more power over our lives than a hurricane. They project from our subconscious, creating our lives around us as if they were a movie projector creating images on a 360 degree screen. If you grow up believing (not just wishing strongly) that you will get into business, you will. If you grow up believing that nobody can get a job these days, you won't. We are a mass of countless beliefs, many overlapping, adding, subtracting, working for us, working against us. And we're only aware of a few of them.

Do the following beliefs sound familiar? *I'm no good at speaking in public; I always get flustered in front of a group; I'm useless without my notes.* Many people are severely handicapped in life by the simple belief that they cannot speak easily in front of an audience. Beliefs create reality. Few beliefs are so worthy of change. And few beliefs are so easy to change.

The subconscious does not distinguish truth from untruth.
It simply carries out the instructions you give it.

That's how it got the beliefs in the first place. And that's how you change them. Sportspeople know it well and thousands of top performers cross the finishing line first having already rehearsed it a hundred times in their heads. Visualisation feeds the subconscious a new picture of the self. Whether or not the new picture is 'real' is irrelevant. The subconscious adjusts its belief programming and simply creates the new reality. The old saying goes, what man can conceive, he can achieve.

Program your subconscious to start turning you into an excellent speaker.

Unrealistic? Unscientific? Just imagination? Not at all. Most scientists in my workshops — and I've had hundreds — willingly accept the reality of the exercise.

Albert Einstein had these views of imagination and reality: 'Imagination is more important than knowledge', and 'Propositions arrived at by purely logical means are completely devoid of reality'. Einstein knew how to open the tap from his subconscious.

He then applied logic to what came out.

I have seen individuals begin workshops unable to face a group without a tremor in the hands and voice, and end workshops able to face aggressive, 'loaded' audiences with unshakeable confidence, authority and conviction. In all cases the ability was already there, only waiting for the trainees to rid themselves of internal barriers. They transformed their beliefs and self-image. Their self-esteem hitched a ride. Why not try Activity 1 (Chapter 7, page 115) and see whether it helps you?

So, as we get into the principles of *Making Presentations Happen* I urge you to think big about your potential. Anything less is a chain round your ankle. You cannot gain beyond your own expectations.

chapter 2

Thinking the right way

- Choosing to become an excellent communicator

- Making the three life choices

- Working out your personal performance key

'We ask ourselves, "Who am I to be brilliant, gorgeous, talented, fabulous?" Actually, who are you not to be? ... As we let our own light shine, we unconsciously give other people permission to do the same. As we are liberated from our own fear, our presence automatically liberates others.'
From Nelson Mandela's 1994 inaugural speech

Often, far and away the best start you can make to accomplishing something is deciding to do so. This is very true of becoming a first-rate presenter or public speaker. It has all the simplicity and obviousness of the wheel ...

■ CHOOSING TO BECOME AN EXCELLENT COMMUNICATOR

Do you see how cunning this is? You can't make such a decision and still cling to limiting negative beliefs about your abilities.

Look in the mirror. Choose to become an excellent communicator everywhere: with live audiences, at work, in the media, on social occasions, at home with your closest life companions. Even if you're only considering work, what other choice is there? The days are long gone when a manager, team leader or supervisor could simply issue memos from behind closed doors.

Recently, our managing director took the lift in our building, sharing it with a young executive from another company in the same building. They introduced themselves.

'You people teach presentation skills, don't you?' she said.

'Yes, we do.'

'I've avoided public speaking all my life', she said. 'I can't do role-plays, I just get incredibly nervous. But now I'm the manager in my branch and I'm expected to talk to clients regularly. It's my first presentation on Saturday. It's to 200 people. I need some help.'

She did the training with us. We saw her speaking at the event she had feared, and she was very good. No, she was extremely good, a delight to watch and listen to. Then, a few weeks later, she and the MD met up, again by accident, again in the lift.

'You know, you guys have changed my life!' she exclaimed.

'Really?'

'I was so nervous about public speaking and now I'm taking every opportunity to do it. I just love it.'

Our MD came into the office with a 1000 watt glow of satisfaction. But his glow faded slightly as he realised something. We hadn't changed her life. She had. Yes, we had had an influence, but not the crucial one. The most vital ingredient was clearly her ability to choose her way. She chose to follow up the chance meeting. She chose to learn to speak in public. She chose to become an excellent communicator.

I urge you to use your ability to choose in the same way. Abraham Lincoln would have understood. He said, 'Success is not a matter of spontaneous combustion. You have to set yourself alight.'

■ MAKING THE THREE LIFE CHOICES

This section is the core of the book. These choices go way beyond the immediate target of speaking to live audiences.

LIFE CHOICE 1
Choose your attitude to any circumstance.

> You can't choose your feelings about any event — they come from your history and your mix of beliefs about life. You can choose your attitude and response to the event — they are your creation right now and can profoundly change the event itself.

If the data projector breaks down do you feel embarrassed? If the audience dislikes your message, do you feel nervous? If an interjector throws a loaded curve ball at you do you feel that you're on the back foot?

One of the worst excesses of pop psychology last century was the idea that to avoid becoming shrink fodder you should always 'be yourself'. Whatever you felt in one instant was 'you' and had to be acted out. So it became almost a duty to express those feelings, which simply arrived, imposed themselves as 'you' and started directing your movie.

A little matter was overlooked. Regardless of your feelings, you still have an infinite number of choices on what attitude you'll adopt and how you'll respond. Soldiers in the trenches under fire would all feel the fear, but responses could range from fleeing to attacking. Ten per cent of life is what happens to you, 90 per cent is your attitude to what happens to you.

Here's someone well qualified to say that we can, indeed, choose our attitude and response to any circumstance.

'We who lived in concentration camps can remember the men who walked through the huts comforting others, giving away their last piece of bread. They offer sufficient proof that everything can be taken from a man but one last thing: the last of the human freedoms — to choose one's attitude in any given set of circumstances, to choose one's own way.' Victor Frankl, psychiatrist

If that was possible, then we can certainly choose how we react to events in our everyday lives, including our presentations.

LIFE CHOICE 2
Choose to get out of your head ... and into theirs.

> Depart from your own fears by focusing most of your attention

on their needs and concerns. Choose to be there for your
audience more than for yourself.

An audience has a collective need for the speaker to get out of his or her own head and show some understanding of us. And yet how many of us — the moment we step in front of an audience — become concerned only with ourselves *I'm no good at this . . . I'll forget my words . . . I look awkward . . . This is embarrassing . . .* etc. If you allow that self-conscious commentator to be loud and continuous in your head, you will guarantee the very thing you fear: that you will not be a good presenter.

Instead, you'll set out to meet people's eyes, with an expression that shows you're interested in how your message is going down with them. That concern becomes a continuous rapport with the audience in which you sense or feel their collective state. It's as if part of you is out there with the audience, able to monitor the collective mind.

I'm sure you can see that this goes well beyond speaking in public. Whoever you speak to, you can get out of your own head by focusing on that person; in the sense of their needs, concerns and feelings. The rewards are beyond measure.

LIFE CHOICE 3
Choose to be comfortable with people's feelings and concerns.

Treat feelings and facts differently. Always accept feelings — they
cannot be judged, they simply exist — though you may reject the way
they are expressed. Reject or accept facts assertively as you see them.

A local body CEO told me he was sitting at his office desk one day, when he heard a commotion. He put his head out of the door to see what was happening. And there, coming down the corridor, was an elderly man waving a stick and a rates demand. He was shouting abuse, staff were trying unsuccessfully to stop him, and he was heading for the CEO.

At this point, it might have been appropriate to threaten the man with calling the police if he didn't calm down. Instead, the CEO applied life choice 3.

'What's the matter?' he asked (tone neutral but concerned).

If anything the shouting got louder, and was accompanied by accusations and finger stabbing at the CEO's chest.

'Well,' the CEO said, 'if I thought that, I'd be angry too. Come and sit down and we'll see what we can sort out.'

Not bad, is it? Let's be in no doubt about why. First, there's the word 'angry', which shows that the CEO was willing to put a name to the elderly man's feeling, accepting and acknowledging it without judgement even though he might shortly be arguing against the man's facts or logic. Second, and much more subtle, he simply chose to be comfortable in the face of the anger.

Throughout the rest of this book, you'll see the three life choices drifting in the background, waiting for you to pick them up.

■ WORKING OUT YOUR PERSONAL PERFORMANCE KEY

Have you ever given a presentation while trying to remember a list of instructions about how to give a presentation? It doesn't work. But what if you had one phrase — a very special personal prod you could give yourself before and during — that would open up glittering presentations to live audiences?

- In this section you'll select your own trial personal performance key.
- In the near future you'll refine or change your performance key.
- In the years ahead, if you work at it now, your key will become a natural part of you and you won't even have to think about it.

FINDING YOUR PERSONAL KEY TO FLOW

The steps in Figure 2.1 represent principles of communication. They're certainly necessary, but what's really going to count for you is the doorway, which symbolises opening the way to what psychologists call 'flow'. Flow is a state of mind. When you enter flow, the words come easily, time flies, you feel exhilarated and in perfect control.

Getting an intellectual understanding of the principles will do little for you. Unlocking flow is the single greatest skill you can extract from this book. The door can be opened with several different keys. It happens that the keys closely resemble a few of the principles of communication, and one of them is likely to lead you to flow.

Don't try to learn the keys like a bullet list. They are only keys, and maybe only one — or a variation — will suit you. They're not exclusive, they're just popular as starting points. Once you have found your trial key, you can and should alter the wording to suit you. For example, the first key is Let go of the bush. I'll explain that shortly, but for now it's enough to know that it refers to releasing fears. One trainee, a firm believer in the Bible, changed the wording to Get out of the boat — a reminder of Jesus telling Peter to release his fear, get out of the boat and walk on water.

There is no one way to describe it that would succeed with everyone. Try each of the following keys. See if you can find one, or a variation on one, that will lead you to great presentation performance.

And remember, however you word it, your performance key will only have value for you as a feeling or attitude. In this part, deliberately give your intellect second place to your feelings — or instinct. Peter Ustinov said it, albeit tongue in cheek, 'The duty of intelligence is merely to correct the instinct in cases of emergency'.

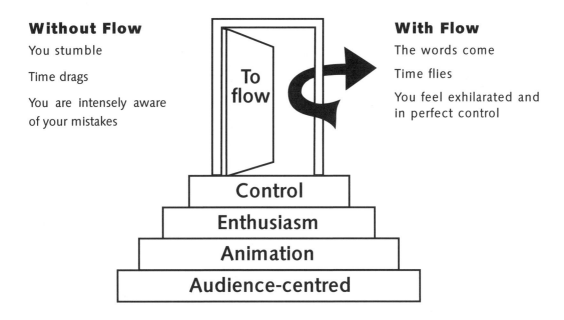

FIGURE 2.1
Going through to 'flow'

Without Flow

You stumble

Time drags

You are intensely aware of your mistakes

To flow

With Flow

The words come

Time flies

You feel exhilarated and in perfect control

Control

Enthusiasm

Animation

Audience-centred

■ FIVE POPULAR STARTERS

For this section it's important to do Activities 2 to 9 in Chapter 7. I urge you to throw heart and soul into them. The reality is that if you just read the theory you'll understand more but your skill level won't rise. High quality research (an average of several studies by the Association of Research Libraries) has found that:

- we retain just 10 per cent of what we read
- we retain 70 per cent of what we talk over with others
- we retain 80 per cent of what we use and do.

Here's the first performance key you might choose for unlocking flow.

1. LET GO OF THE BUSH!
I'm going to release my fears and fly.

There was once a man who had a couple too many at the local. On the way home he found himself lost. Having negotiated his way into obstacles using the Lord's name as his compass, he finally fell over a cliff 1000 feet high. But a little way down the cliff face, he just managed to grasp hold of a bush.

So there he is, hanging, 50 feet from the top, 950 feet to the rocks and sea below. So he calls out towards the top of the cliff, 'Help! Help! Is there anyone there?'

'God here,' a voice booms down to him, 'Just let go of the bush: believe, and you will be saved.'

He considers this. He looks up, he looks down, he looks straight ahead. Then he calls up to the top of the cliff.

'Is there anyone else up there?'

It's the letting go that's relevant here. Let the bush represent the bundle of doubts and anxieties that make us grasp the false security of speaking in monotones and officialese, and talking to pieces of paper rather than people.

You know those anxieties, don't you? — *Am I going to forget the words? Did I remember to brush my hair? I hope I don't drop my notes ... I'm standing awkwardly ... I can't seem to focus on anyone ... They don't understand a thing I say ... Maybe I should move around ... I'm speaking too fast again ... My ears stand out ... They're all looking at my ears ... Am I speaking in a monotone?* etc., etc., etc.

To allow a litany like that into your head when you're trying to make a presentation is like allowing a herd of elephants to weed the lettuces. You get a very flat and indigestible salad. And yet you can't fight such destructive self-talk point by point because each is generated from the level of attitude and belief. Beat it by working directly on the attitude and belief. So here's the method that works for many.

Tell yourself in internally reverberating tones: LET GO OF THE BUSH! It's an act of faith in yourself! The biggest risk in life is to take no risks, and that is certainly true of presentations. The time to take a risk is now. It's like thinking, *Well, if I hang here I'm dead anyway. I've got nothing to lose.* Now you have no alternative but to fly; release your fears, allow yourself to fly. Now your focus can change from yourself and your own fears, and turn instead to your audience.

This particular key works so dramatically for some trainees that it seems more like a switch.

Have a go at Activity 2 (Chapter 7, page 116). What was your gut reaction? Does the idea of letting go of the bush excite you? Or does it leave you totally unmoved? Somewhere in between? Keep the feeling in mind for comparison with the other keys.

Re-word?

If *Let go of the bush* looks like a good key for you, how could you re-word it to make it more suitable for yourself? Here are some examples that others have chosen:

Let go!	Walk on water!
Let go and go for it!	Walk on air!
Fly!	Drop Linus's blanket!

Your call. But just one word of caution. Don't end up with the word 'don't' in a performance key. A negative key — such as *Don't cling to my fears* — is likely to reinforce poor performance. Imagine what happens if you say to a child, 'You can have an ice-cream if you can last five minutes without thinking about elephants'.

Here's another performance key you might choose.

2. GET OUT OF MY HEAD!
I'll be audience-centred, changing from an inward focus on myself and my worries, to an outward focus on looking after my audience.

Does it look familiar? Yes, it's Life Choice No. 2. For many people this acts as a personal performance key in its own right.

It does not mean that you should be audience-centred in the sense of fear of the audience — that's *self*-centred. You're stuck in your own head if you stay inwardly focused, usually on your own nervousness. You're wallowing in your own head if you give the audience jargon they don't know, if you talk the language of officialese and legalese, if you read a monotonal speech word-for-word, or if you talk to dead pieces of paper rather than to live people.

All of us have a voice in our head that provides a self-conscious commentary. *I'm no good at this ... I'm terrified by pauses ... They'll see the egg on my tie ... I forgot to do my hair ... I'm moving awkwardly ... They're all looking at me ... How can I get through this? I'm so self-conscious ...* and so on.

But if you have been truly 'out of your own head' — away from that destructive inner voice — the audience will feel an empathy with you that is almost tangible. They'll leave saying things like, 'Well I don't agree with her, but I can see her point of view. You've got to admire her style'.

The bonus
Get out of your own head! is a highly successful personal key for those who suffer most from public speaking anxiety.

> **The more you make yourself audience-centred,
> the easier it is to manage nervousness.**

That's so important, let me pursue it with some emotional blackmail. To allow yourself to be so self-conscious that you become a self-effacing bundle of nerves is self-indulgence that cuts off your audience! In my workshops I might say something like this to a trainee: 'If you stay self-conscious you're insulting your audience by putting your needs before theirs'. You have no choice. Stay self-centred and you'll lose them. But come out of yourself, out of your own head, meet the audience warmly, put them first by tuning in to what they need, and they will be yours. It's as if the more you give yourself to the audience, the more you give to yourself.

Ironic, isn't it? You serve your own needs best by putting the audience's needs before your own. When you practise it speaking to others, the personal reward is instantaneous!

'There was a man, though some did count him mad. The more he cast away the more he had.' W.S. Plummer

Now would be a good time to do Activity 3 (Chapter 7, page 117). How were you at imagining yourself getting out of your own head? How was your gut reaction, compared with that of the first key?

Re-word?
How might you re-word this key to improve it for you? Here are some examples others have chosen:

Get into the heads of the audience!   Get into them!
Get out!   Look after them!
Them, not me!

A cautionary tale
There's a folklore story about the Coca Cola company when it first went into China. They wanted a Chinese word that sounded like Coca Cola. The translator gave them one and the firm was pleased. But they neglected one little thing: what the word meant to the audience! To Mandarin-speaking Chinese it meant, 'Bite the wax tadpole'.

Don't feed your audiences the wax tadpole! How do you feed them the wax tadpole? By forgetting them in the preparation. By ignoring how they perceive and feel things. By giving them carefully crafted jargon, officialese and legalese, by reading a monotonal speech word-for-word, and by talking to dead pieces of paper rather than to live people!

Let's look at another performance key you might choose.

3. TALK TO REAL PEOPLE!
I'll think of the audience as individuals and talk to each one.

Prosecution: When he went, had you gone and had she — if she wanted to and were able, for the time being excluding all the restraints on her not to go — gone also, would he have brought you, meaning you and she, with him to the station?
Defence: Objection! The question should be taken out and shot.
(Richard Lederer, *Disorder in the Court*)

Are you someone who talks to audiences like a trance medium speaking in tongues? Think carefully before you say no, this phenomenon is endemic! Imagine this. You rise from your seat, you face the audience, you open your mouth and you intend to say: 'Morning everyone. Thank you for the chance to explain what my project team has been up to.' Instead, you listen in amazement as your subconscious causes your tongue to spew forth a foreign language: 'I would like at this point in time and on behalf of Coma Inducement Limited to express my sincere appreciation for your generosity in allowing me this opportunity to address the topic of the projected and actual outcomes of the project carried out by the team I am currently facilitating.'

Who needs sleeping pills when you can listen to presenters like that?

Actually, it's no joke. Countless presenters report a feeling of impersonal detachment and can see and hear themselves performing formal, tortuous, verbal acrobatics around what should be direct and simple. Worse: very often that language is delivered in a monotone, without a trace of human warmth! Strangest of all, many have told me that under the influence of that strange feeling, they have come out with phrases and words they have never used before, and would never normally use on human beings!

How rich the irony is. Such atrocious performances often happen because we are afraid of giving a bad performance! The fear is itself the enemy and it speaks in our skulls like this: 'Oh no, I'm speaking to an audience!' But you're not speaking to an audience. You're speaking to people, real people. Next time you suspect yourself of delivering the language of the little green men visiting Earth, ask yourself the corridor test question:

How would I say this if I met just one of these people in the corridor?

That test alone can transform speeches from detached, stuffy and jargon-filled to simple, personal, direct and more authoritative. Speaking to real people is an outrageously simple and effective idea. Have a go at Activity 4 (Chapter 7, page 118) to make sure you pass the test.

Sometimes I meet the objection that if the occasion is important it must be wrong to speak informally. Not so. The issue here is an evil I call the *language of importance.*

A government department official at a workshop we held (I'll call him Jack) was in front of a group of fellow officials, role-playing himself explaining new regulations to members of the public. I awaken the camera. The red light winks. Jack begins.

'Good afternoon, ladies and gentlemen. I would like to take advantage of this opportunity to express what a pleasure and honour it is to be invited to address you today ... ' Jack is expressing this ineffable pleasure directly to his prompt notes in a low monotone. Already he has induced a look of disillusionment in his listeners, detectable by the sagging in the muscles around their cheeks. He continues. 'You may rest assured that the department maintains a multi-faceted, multi-level monitoring system on all dealings with the public and, in fact, anyone who has

indicated dissatisfaction. It has necessitated a re-evaluation of service so as to maximise efficiency, and in so doing, significantly improve . . . '

'Wait, wait!' I kill the red light. The 'laymen' have gone glassy-eyed and slack-jawed. Their arms hang lifelessly down the sides of the chairs. If this gobbledygook continues, some of them will start to dribble. The challenge is to explain it to Jack. I say, 'If you were a layman listening to you, would you want to be addressed as "the public"?'

'Why not?' he asks.

'But wouldn't you just want to be addressed as "you"?'

Jack looks sceptical.

'Okay. Listen to your words.' I play the tape back to him. 'You hear how many very long sentences and formal words you're using?'

'Of course. What's wrong with it? It's important material.'

One of the 'public' breaks in. 'Jack, ease up a bit. The simple stuff is better.'

Actually, Jack does understand what's being said. His last phrase was the clue. And he explains his unease by talking about something deeply and genuinely felt by many officials in all walks of life. 'If I talk in simple language, it will sound unimportant and I'll lose credibility.'

All right, there's only one thing for it: the corridor test. 'Jack, imagine that you met one of the "laymen" here out in the corridor and you used that language: what would that person think?'

Silence. Then Jack nods. 'He'd think I've got screws that need tightening.'

So there it is again: with some occasions excepted, the fact that individuals have assembled as an audience should make not one jot of difference to your language.

On most speaking occasions, every individual wants you to speak in the same verbal language you would use if you were chatting to them in the corridor. Allow for the rest of the audience only in your vocal and visual languages.

You may hold an important title or rank, but your credibility with an audience has nothing whatever to do with the language of importance. It has everything to do with your ability to speak person to person. The language of real people.

However, you must also be real to yourself. Some speakers falsely adopt the colloquialisms of their audience in an effort to get on their side. It's a terrible mistake. The falseness is instantly transparent and audiences promptly award a credibility rating of zero. If you doubt me, watch closely next time an adult talks 'children talk' to your five-year-old, or pats the child on the head.

The language of real people is your own, in its simplest, plainest, most direct and unaffected form. Speak that language and you may be surprised how easy it is to bridge cultural gaps.

Here's a little tool to help you put the concept into practice: use the words 'you' or 'we' to an audience, as if talking to a single person.

If you're an accountant and you sit in an audience of 2000 accountants at an accountants' convention, would you rather have a speaker say, 'Accountants must sell their own services in order to survive' or speak to you directly: 'If you want to survive you have to sell your own services', or 'If we want to survive . . . ', etc.?

'Nothing gets in the way of doing business more than language that is anything other than conversational.' Granville N. Toogood, *The Articulate Executive*

Try Activity 5 (Chapter 7 page 119) — it's a good way to find out if you're talking to real people or not.

Re-word?
How might you personalise the wording of the *Talk to real people!* key to make it right for you? Here are some examples others have chosen:

Get real!   Break it down!
Talk to individuals!   Walk in the corridor!

Remember, the personal performance key is little use if it is treated as a dispassionate, intellectual concept. The exclamation marks are there to remind you to deliberately invoke a feeling. Develop attitude.

Here's another performance key you might choose.

4. PASS THE PASSION TEST!
I'll show appropriate enthusiasm. I'll be keen to explain. I'll be passionate. I'll be warm and enjoy myself.

'Nothing great was ever achieved without enthusiasm.' Ralph Waldo Emerson

The trainees who get the most out of this key are usually those who are surprised when I stop the camera and ask them this question.
'Tell me, are you interested in this topic?'
'Of course I am' they reply, surprised.
'Are you enthusiastic about the subject?'
'Yes!' Indignant. It's their favourite subject. Am I deaf and blind? Do I have an attention deficit problem?
'I don't know that. You haven't *shown* it.'
'But . . . ' The speaker looks for support to their colleagues, only to find shaking heads. Grinning, but shaking. 'Uh-uh.'

So many have difficulty with that gap in perception, it's worth spelling out what to do about it. The first way is to take the key *Pass the passion test!* at face value. Some people spot that phrase and need little more. Another way to put a hand on the key is with the phrase *keenness to explain*. For some, the idea that you must show your keenness to explain is so graphic it becomes their own re-wording of the performance key.

Show that you are keen to explain.

It's often a big step to boost your performance like this. So I will often say, 'For a moment, don't be yourself. Act the part instead. Act at being a presenter who is enthusiastic about their topic. Act it just up to the level where you think it's "over the top"'.

Act the part of a presenter with the appropriate level of passion. Then let the real you catch up.

The next attempt at presenting is often a beauty. The interesting thing is that having spoken in public with more enthusiasm and animation then ever before, the trainee often knows it was good and that the fear of being 'over the top' was unfounded.

But for those who don't see it immediately, there's often a delightful exchange.

'What do you think?' I will ask.

'No. It was too much. I was uncomfortable.'

Their own colleagues promptly and vehemently deny it. 'No it wasn't. It was good. Never seen you do it so well.' And then I replay the tape so they can see for themselves. At that moment I watch the trainee more than the screen. I'm looking for the slow nod as they accept that this new picture of themselves is viable for the future. Their comfort threshold has shifted.

Here's another way to look at it.

Show appropriate warmth, by showing that you're enjoying the company of the audience.

I don't mean a smile from the lips. Turn that on all the time and you'll be like the waitress who begins an evening with a flash of teeth. 'Good evening. My name is Sharlene. I am your waitress for the evening', giving the real message (remember the 93 per cent) that she would rather catch smallpox than serve you. I'm talking about warmth from the eyes, with or without the smile. Try Activity 6 (Chapter 7, page 120) to find out how to gauge the difference.

Of course, you can't switch on warmth you don't have. Audiences take about a microsecond to x-ray the cheese. But it's equally disastrous to turn off the natural warmth you do have and that is by far the most common sin. Time and again I see beginner trainees turn their natural warmth off the second they begin to perform, and then turn it on again the second they finish.

Showing natural warmth brings out some of the most spectacular changes in trainee presenters. When asked to analyse the difference, their colleagues use words like, 'Better presence, more authority, more confidence, more at ease. More believable somehow.'

A Chinese scientist came to one of the workshops. For half a day she struggled, partly because English was difficult for her, but mostly because she was self-conscious about her heavy accent. The self-consciousness kept her constantly on the back foot. Then she hit on a subject in which she at last dared to show appropriate enthusiasm. She role-played giving a welcoming speech to a group of visitors to her house, and it was very important to her that visitors feel welcome. She allowed her enthusiasm to overwhelm all vestiges of self-consciousness. And it showed, in the same way the sun breaks through departing rain clouds. She was so warm, so open-hearted, that when she finished there was a stunned silence before considerable applause.

We had missed some of her accented words, but we had not missed a single nuance of the heart of her speech.

The bonus

It's the same bonus as with being audience-centred. Adopting this performance key helps you put fear in its place.

> **Enthusiasm burns off excess nervous energy.**

Re-word?

Could you use the concept *Pass the passion test!*? Activity 7 (Chapter 7, page 121) will help you check whether your passion is noticeable. How might you word it to personalise it to yourself? Here are some wordings others have chosen:

Be keen to explain!	Show my enthusiasm!
Act passionate!	The three bears!
Act the part!	Rumplestiltskin!
Show that I care!	Speak with my heart!

Here's another performance key you might like to adopt.

5. MOVE ONTO THE FRONT FOOT!

I'm going to take control of the message, the audience and the situation.

This popular performance key is unique in that many literally shift their weight onto the front foot to jump-start the attitude change. The original meaning came from hand-to-hand combat where the fighter on the front foot is the one in control.

The surprise is that in front of an audience, our body language agrees with the metaphor. When we are on the back foot, when we're defensive, or just trying to struggle through and survive, many of us do, literally, incline slightly backwards. When we are front- or forward-footed in our thinking, when we have a feeling of being in control of the situation, many of us do, literally, incline forward. This is just as true for sitting; an incline forward to signify increased intensity, involvement and control.

Carrying out the physical action can help you achieve the mental attitude. And, of course, it is the mental attitude that counts, regardless of whether you're sitting or standing.

Many presenters adopt a back-footed mental attitude right from the beginning. Typical would be, 'Might as well get it over with.' Or a self-effacing opening phrase, like, 'I'm not much at making speeches, so I'll be brief.' Such presenters are reinforcing their own fears and creating self-fulfilling prophecies. It is the human equivalent of the submissive behaviour of many animals when backing down from a threat.

Does that thought annoy or shock you? I hope so, because the feeling is useful for change. Not only do we need to eliminate all such signals, we need to go onto the front foot to achieve the opposite affect.

1. Recognise that you are on the back foot. There are many signs: you might feel that you're not 'connecting' with the audience, you might feel mentally distanced from them, or threatened that they don't like your message, or by their expressions of boredom.

2. Recognise that you can choose to change the situation.

3. Command yourself with the key. Say to yourself, 'Enough of that! Now I'll move onto the front foot, taking control of myself and the situation'.

4. Move — physically, then mentally. Make your whole body language move first, then take your determination with it. If you're standing, shift your weight forward slightly — literally onto the forward foot or onto the balls of your feet. If you're sitting, incline further forward with straight upper back, perhaps with forearms on the table. In either case, follow through by looking the audience in the eye, increasing your energy level and intensity, showing your determination and keenness to get the message across. Let your upper body and arms move freely to emphasise your points. Let your facial muscles move freely.

Activity 8 (Chapter 7, page 122) is a checklist to help you move onto the front foot.

Re-word?

How do you feel about this performance key? How might you word it to personalise it for yourself? Here are some wordings others have chosen:

Move and take charge!	Incline forward!
I'm in control!	Body, head, eyes, forward!

Take control!   Get forward, get interested!
Lean into it!

'OPEN SESAME'

I have put emphasis on feelings and attitudes as opposed to intellect. In fact, if you haven't explored your own gut-level responses, I urge you to go back, buy another ticket and take the ride again.

For Ali Baba there was one treasure and one key phrase: *Open sesame.* For you, as a presenter, there is only one *attitude,* but it can take many names. You need one that works for you.

chapter 3

Doing the groundwork

- Winning over your audience before you see them

- Designing successful presentations

- Knowing how and when to use audiovisual aids

'It usually takes me more than three weeks to prepare a good impromptu speech.'
Mark Twain

When it comes to preparing to give a presentation, remember the first personal power: *connected* personal power. When you prepare directly for such connection, you'll be preparing to generate these thoughts and feelings in your audience:

- This presenter 'knows where I'm coming from'. He or she understands me.
- This content is relevant to me.
- This presenter is 'straight down the line'. I can trust him or her.
- This presenter respects me, even though I may not agree with him or her.
- This is a first rate presenter.

■ WINNING OVER YOUR AUDIENCE BEFORE YOU SEE THEM

Your presentation will start for you long before you stand up to speak. If you cover most of the bases discussed in the following pages you'll be able to maximise your effect on your audience — and make it seem effortless.

ASK THE HOW/WHAT/WHERE QUESTIONS

If you don't know the answers to these, you'll need to find out:

- *How long do I speak?* Little planning is possible if you don't know. If you're calling the shots, tell the organiser what you anticipate.
- *Is food involved?* If you eat a four-course dinner on the way to the function, the last thing you want to discover is a five-course dinner at the function before you speak.
- *Are there any curtains?* Many a presentation has foundered at the start gun because nobody thought to check until the presenter turned up with the slide projector.
- *What are the alcohol arrangements?* If the audience is going to be well lubricated you had better modify your speech on interesting parallels between Eastern religion and spin polarity in quantum mechanics.
- *What's the audience going to be wearing?* That's the way to find out what you'll wear. As a general rule, dress the same or slightly better than the audience. What's at stake here is how the audience perceives your respect for them. If you do ask what you should wear, be wary of the organiser who tells you disarmingly, 'Oh, just anything, it doesn't matter'. Not at all helpful if you turn up in jeans to find the audience in corporate wear.
- *How big is the audience?* This may affect amplification and microphone arrangement.
- *What audiovisual aids are available?* If they're complex, do you have technical back-up? Will you need time to rehearse with them?
- *What else will be happening?* What else will the audience experience at that gathering? Modifications might be necessary if your post-modernist perspective of Icelandic syntax comes right after the belly dancing.
- *Who has spoken to them in the past?* Is this audience used to light-hearted banter or highbrow intellectualism?

- *Who is speaking immediately before you and what are their topics?* The answer might subtly affect your content.
- *What is the official title for your speech or presentation?* That's by no means trivial. If your specialty is, 'How you can stop sheep-dog viruses destroying your farm in one season', but you've been given the title 'A discussion on sheep dogs and micro-organisms', you might find there's no-one there to listen.
- *What are the financial arrangements?* Not always appropriate, of course. But if it is, now is the time. If you're uncomfortable with asking, or bargaining, you might have to hire an agent.

ASK THE CRUNCH AUDIENCE QUESTIONS

You start winning your audience right here. The whole scope of your preparation and structure, and the tone you adopt will be affected by the answers.

- *What kind of people will be there?* What gender? What professions? What interests? Will the individuals in the audience know each other? Are they all members of the same group? The answers can tell you a lot about the atmosphere you can expect. How sophisticated are they? How literate are they? What's the level of expertise? That'll tell you even more about the level of jargon that's acceptable. The fine details of printed circuit boards might be fascinating to electronics engineers, but would cause an audience of electronics salespeople to vanish before your eyes.
- *What do they know about the topic already?* Are they all armed with the latest knowledge? Do they know nothing about it? Is there a mixture? Very often there's a mixture of expertise and you'll have to take that into account, so as not to oscillate between sounding condescending and boring.
- *Will there be anyone who knows more about the topic, or parts of it, than you?* If the answer is yes, see Chapter 5, page 95, 'When there's an expert in the audience'.
- *Why will the audience be there, and what do they expect from you?* Are they there willingly? Do they have a passing level of interest already or will they be there under orders?

And above all ...
- *What do they feel about the topic already?* When you find the answers to this question you'll begin one of the most powerful components of persuasion: pre-empting objections and concerns. Ask these kind of questions:

    What are the predominant audience feelings about the topic?

    Is the audience entrenched? What proportion?

    Is the audience divided? In what proportion?

    How many people are undecided?

    What's the worst question the audience is likely to ask?

The answers can and should drastically affect your preparation. Suppose, for example, you're planning to tell them about some wonderful new software, but last time they got new software, half your audience were treated for paranoia and the rest applied for early retirement. Will knowing that affect your preparation?

■ THE FOUR-STEP ALL-PURPOSE PREPARATION (THE CITY MODEL)

What you'll need: an ordinary black pen, a packet of coloured felt pens, a blank sheet of paper (your brainstorm page), a copy of the Delivery Form (see Chapter 7, page 131) and normal research sources for factual content.

And here's a preview of THE CITY MODEL:

1. Write the city-view sentence

2. Brainstorm and research

3. Structure — connect your ideas

4. Organise your ideas

The method handles virtually all types of presentation. It's going to be explained in full, to cope with formal, career-on-the-line presentations or speeches. But it is essentially simple. For short, informal speeches you'll find it easy to drop the formal parts.

The thought of standing before an audience unprepared terrifies many people. But despite Mark Twain's witticism, there's no need to endure agony when preparation can be easy and effective.

It's based on what I call the city model of a presentation or speech: the streets are the details, the suburbs are the major sections and the city-view (or overview) is what the whole thing is about, *including your real purpose with the audience*. I'll explain that shortly. For now, just glance ahead a little to get used to the model as well as a little jargon.

Here are the terms we'll use:

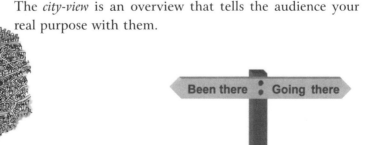

The *city-view* is an overview that tells the audience your real purpose with them.

A *signpost* tells the audience where you are in your presentation.

A *suburb* is a label you give to any section of your presentation.

A *street* is any detail in your presentation.

A *spotlight* is a detail selected for special emphasis at the beginning or end of your presentation.

step ①   **WRITE THE CITY-VIEW SENTENCE**

This is the most crucial part of the whole preparation. It's the time to get to the point. To come right out and say it. To say the end at the beginning. It's an overview written to express *your real purpose with the audience*. For one presentation, you must have one purpose, one message. It will be the core of your introduction, though probably not the first thing you say. Ask yourself, 'What do I want my audience to think, feel or do as a result of my presentation?'

Use the city-view generator:

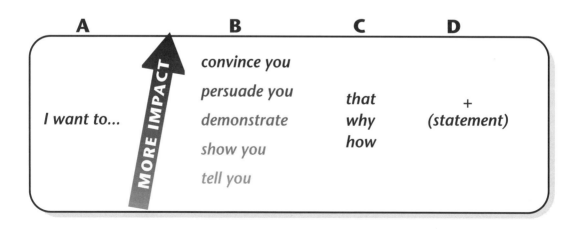

A	B	C	D
	convince you		
	persuade you	that	+
I want to...	demonstrate	why	(statement)
MORE IMPACT	show you	how	
	tell you		

EXAMPLE:

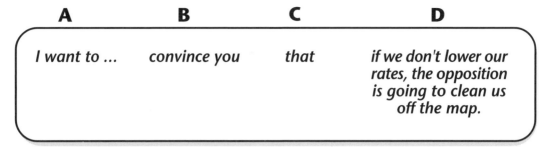

A	**B**	**C**	**D**
I want to …	*convince you*	*that*	*if we don't lower our rates, the opposition is going to clean us off the map.*

A. The words 'I want' acknowledge that it's you on the line, not your topic.

B. The higher you go on this list, the more powerful you will be as a presenter.

Powerful presenters take a position, adopt a stance.
They do not try to be (or pretend to be) objective.

Of course, some topics must be exceptions. Audiences often want to (or want to pretend to) make up their own minds based simply on a set of facts you present to them. In that case, you are bound to go to the bottom of the list, using words like show and tell: 'I want to show you the facts behind the crisis so you can make up your own minds where we go from here.' But be warned, many presenters choose the lower end of the list, fooling themselves with the word objectivity when their underlying and real motive is to play safe, avoid criticism, avoid putting themselves on the line — undermining their own personal authority.

C. The word 'that'. One small word, one giant leap forward in your ability to hook your audience. Think carefully before you use the words 'why' and 'how' because they usually convey an intention to deal only with facts. For example, 'I want to show you how the schedule works.' Facts alone can often be boring. Ask yourself, 'Can I make my purpose stronger?'

D. The reason you're there. Remember to make it personal and audience-centred. For example, ' … that increasing taxes benefits you in the long run' works much better than ' … that increasing taxes is a good thing'.

Warning! Have you noticed that the city-view generator doesn't allow you to use the word 'about'? That's because 'I'm going to talk about … ' tells the audience that you're going to have a safe academic detached discussion in which you personally are not on the line.

Even worse is the stuffy phrase, 'My topic is . . . ', which has the same effect as administering a powerful sedative to your audience.

Now, here's an example to illustrate what can happen if you don't have a city-view sentence in your introduction.

I was asked to help a few scientists with a practise run for an important national seminar with an audience that would include politicians and fund managers. For the practice session one scientist stood up front and I sat with half a dozen of his fellow specialists. On a highly controversial subject, he started like this:

'I'm going to talk about 1080 poison and the residual effects in animal cells.'

You might say that was fair enough — a clear description of the topic. And he was certainly articulate and skilled with visual aids. Even so, after 10 minutes I was lost, and the expressions of his fellow specialists indicated that they were struggling too.

'Are you wanting to convince us of anything?' I asked.

'Well, yes,' he said, surprised. He flapped his hand at the data as if it was self-explanatory. 'I want to convince you that 1080 poison is still the only viable option.'

Did you pick the word 'that'? The expressions on the faces of his colleagues cleared. To a man and woman they all nodded. Now they had a perspective. Now they knew what he wanted to achieve with them.

Now, using your black pen and the city-view generator, write your own city-view in the centre of your blank sheet of paper (which now becomes the brainstorm page). This gives you the core of your introduction. The rest of the presentation will be developed around the city-view.

step ② BRAINSTORM AND RESEARCH

Brainstorming is a crucial few minutes in the development of a presentation or speech. Many neglect it and rush straight to the normal research sources, grabbing content. But that's like shopping only from what you see in display windows.

Even in the most technical presentations, the best resource is usually our own knowledge and experience, our opinions and feelings.

A typical brainstorm page looks like Figure 3.1. Take a look now. You jot down single words or phrases — just enough to remind you of the idea. There will be content material you can put down immediately, of course. And you can do reasonably well if you also jot down responses to these questions: 'What does the audience feel about this?' and 'How can I make my material relevant to the audience?'

For the best results on your brainstorm page, read on . . .

FIGURE 3.1

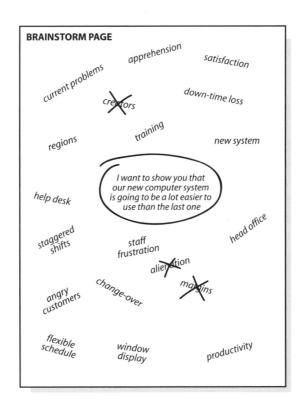

BRAINSTORM PAGE

Pre-empt objections, concerns and related questions

Dealing with objections before they are raised by the audience is one of the most successful ways of convincing or persuading. And it's probably the most powerful of all tools for taking the steam out of a difficult audience.

1. Make a separate list of audience objections, concerns and related feelings.
2. For each objection or concern, ask yourself, 'How could this objection or concern be wrong?'
3. For each that is wrong, use the brainstorm page to jot down a reminder of your answer.
4. For each that is not wrong, use the brainstorm page to jot down an acknowledgment of the point.

Now (or later) you may need to make the following choice about the answers to some objections, concerns or related questions:

EITHER: Articulate it

If you anticipate the objection 'This has got nothing to do with me', you might jot down relevance, and in the speech itself you might meet it in advance starting, 'Now you might be wondering what this has to do with you …'

OR: Don't articulate it but deal with it indirectly

If you anticipate the unspoken concern 'Can I trust this person?' (you), you might jot down 'trust?' and meet it indirectly by talking about contract safeguards.

Prepare to broadcast on WIIFM

You haven't heard of this radio station? But every single member of your audience listens to it constantly. Here it is, spelt out — *What's In It For Me?* And since they're tuned to that station all the time, you would be well advised to broadcast on it. That means preparing to show the specific relevance of your content to that audience.

Very often that will mean using the word 'you'. For example, 'Your computers will handle this stuff, but you'll find them pretty sluggish . . .' Audiences do not sleep when they hear the word 'you'.

Prepare illustrations, metaphors and word pictures

Why? Because if you don't, they won't remember your core message! However worthy, an unsupported general statement has no inherent impact. Such a statement is a code for what is important to you. It might be a concise and convenient code, but audiences don't feel what you feel just by listening to your code. They have to see or hear specific illustrations before they can identify with the feelings involved. Only then will the general statement trigger for them what it triggers for you.

- *Example:* Not just 'This model is structurally sound' but also, 'We laid a concrete slab on it — 642kg — and there was no damage' and also, 'You could run an elephant over it'. (So on your brainstorm page you might jot down 'Concrete', '642kg', 'Elephant'.)
- *Example:* Not just 'We need to change procedures at reception' but also, 'Just last week a woman had to wait 20 minutes in a queue just so she could make a complaint about the length of the queues'. (On your brainstorm page you might jot down 'Cust. 20 mins'.)
- *Example:* Not just 'Cutting prices now would send the wrong signal to our established customers' but also, 'It will be like getting down on our knees and begging.' (On the brainstorm page perhaps write 'Wrong signal, On knees'.)

Of course, making a general statement with passion does help, but not in the way you might think. Audiences are impressed with your feeling for the topic, but that doesn't mean that they have any more feeling for it themselves. You'll still need the illustrations.

Prepare to surprise them!

Be unpredictable. Prepare for ways to surprise them. Here are two effective ways that will boost your impact:

- Don't tell them what they know already. Instead, jot down ideas that acknowledge what they know, and tell them what they don't. For example, 'As most of you know, the schedule changes next week — be especially careful with Day Two.'

- Prepare contrasts, which stimulate feelings in the audience. For example, 'This is not an drain on our resources, but it is an investment in the long-term health and vitality of this firm.'

Look at your city-view sentence. Tell yourself the audience wants you to be *interesting, entertaining* and *memorable*. Now, still with your black pen, swiftly write your ideas all over the brainstorm page, twisting the page to a new angle for each idea. Don't censor or structure. Don't pause. Your mind is never empty. Fly through as many ideas as you can for at least five minutes. Think of yourself as an open tap for ideas. Make sure you:

- jot down ways to pre-empt objections, concerns, related questions. Ask yourself, 'What are the worst questions they could throw at me?'; 'What are the best?'
- jot down ways to broadcast on WIIFM (relating your content to them)
- jot down illustrations, metaphors and word pictures. Anecdotes? Illustrative events? Anything relevant on the news recently? Anything a client has said? A colleague? A child?
- jot down ways of surprising them.

Finished? Did you surprise yourself with the ideas that came? That's the ideal, when the flow of ideas is coming from deep down. By the way, resist any temptation to reject some of the ideas just yet. Don't do that until you are ready to complete the loop.

Now do your normal research from external sources, adding to your brainstorm page as you go: facts and figures, supporting quotes, graphs. You may need to make a phone call or two to research the audience. Add more street details as they occur:

- *Use examples.* Make sure your talk is well endowed with specific, detailed examples. Audiences don't respond to generalities unless they come with illustrations. And don't hesitate to take people 'behind the scenes'. Audiences like the feeling that they're being allowed to peek through normal appearances. Use names, times, colours, textures.
- *Use stories.* Audiences love it. The more specific and detailed the better. Paint pictures with your words. 'Imagine my problem. There I was in an old fashioned stairwell, carved banister, red carpet, moth holes, and I was just . . .'
- *Use quotes.* Make them relevant.

Now you are ready to complete the loop. Go back to your city-view sentence. Do you now want to modify it? If so, you might need to shake down through the steps again. If not, you might want to do a little more brainstorming anyway. Look back through your jottings and ask yourself, 'Is this point relevant to my city-view?' If the answer is no, be ruthless!

Use coloured pens to connect all ideas that belong in the same suburb. Be flexible, change your mind, cross things out, allow for substitutions, deletions and the addition of subsets or 'satellites'. If you see (or can think of) one detail that could be a label for all others of the same colour, put an extra ring around it (or enter it and put two rings around it).

For my example I've got three suburbs. The human mind seems to respond well to that number, but it could easily be two or four, or even one for a very simple talk. If you get to larger numbers — five and up — that's more difficult for audiences to take in. See if you can combine some of them.

FIGURE 3.2
Typical brainstorm page

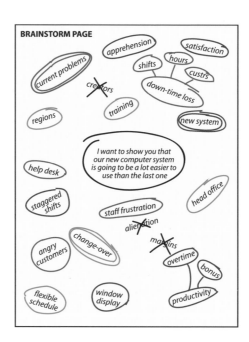

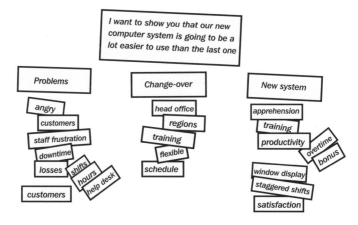

FIGURE 3.3

If you don't care for colours, get a pair of scissors, isolate every detail and connect your ideas by shuffling bits of paper around the desk, as in Figure 3.3. That works just as well.

step 4 ORGANISE YOUR IDEAS

Transfer all information to the Delivery Form (there's a template in Chapter 7, page 131). Modify as you go. Give each column of streets a suburb name (probably using details with double rings). See Figure 3.4.

Now fill in the opening spotlight.

Treat this part lightly at your peril. The average audience takes less than ten seconds to decide if you're going to be worth listening to. Granville Toogood in *The Articulate Executive* (1995) puts it at eight seconds. A documentary study by a group of British psychologists found that interviewers listening to job applicants had irreversibly made up their minds within five seconds.

The opening spotlight is a sentence or more that reaches out to the audience, grabs it by the scruff of its collective shirt and says, 'Get this. What follows is going to be extremely interesting and relevant to you!' You might already have recorded such an idea. If not, think of one.

Figure 3.4
Transferring information to delivery form

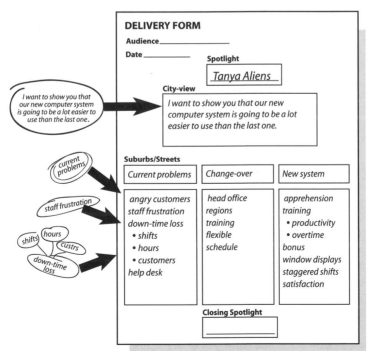

There are two ways to create a spotlight.

EITHER: Establish a common interest with the audience

Tell an anecdote: A small, relevant story. It could be humorous, but never tell an unrelated joke which may raise a laugh, but ends in a let-down. Tradition has it that you tell a joke to relax the audience. Tradition is wrong; usually the one who needs to relax is the speaker.

Get detailed. Get personal. Paint pictures with your words. And make sure the link with your speech is clear. For example, 'Last Tuesday, Sue and I went to see *Love Story* ... yes in the back row. Some decorum please. We were in the middle of the most passionate moment ... no, not our own ... when some idiot up front let off an alarm clock. Well ... [link] I have to tell you that the arrival of competition is the alarm clock for everyone in this room. The honeymoon is over ladies and gentleman. This afternoon I want to ... '

Ask a pointed question: For example, 'How often have you stopped in the middle of some slavery for your boss and said, "There has to be something better than this!"? Well there is. Today I want to ... '

Make a personal statement: For example, 'Ladies and gentlemen. Twenty years ago, I resolved not to touch another cigarette if it killed me. I haven't and it hasn't. This morning I want to ... '

Give them a pointed quote: For example (after scurrilous treatment by the media): 'Morning, folks. "The greatest happiness is to vanquish your enemies, to chase them before you, to rob them of their wealth, to see those dear to them bathed in tears, to clasp to your bosom their wives and daughters." That's Genghis Khan's advice on what we should do to the *Sunday Tattler*. But I suspect the media would consider that a knee jerk reaction, so we need to find another way. In fact I want to ... '

Make a hard-hitting statement: For example, 'Ladies and gentlemen. I have to tell you that if we do not reach agreement tonight, then in six months this branch ... will ... no longer ... exist!'

Give them a stunt: For example, at a weight-watchers convention, a motivation speech might begin with this: 'Anne? Anne Higgins? Ah, there you are'. You leave the stage and head for Anne. (Anne has made significant weight loss and agreed to this.) You sweep her off her feet and hold her high.

OR: Acknowledge the predominant audience mood

Take careful note of this one, especially if you anticipate a difficult audience. It's not showmanship at all — it's quite simply one of the most powerful elements you can put into a presentation, winning the respect of even the most challenging audience.

Ask yourself, 'Does my audience have a major negative feeling about the subject?' If the answer is yes, you may have to use this alternative. For example, 'I know many of you would rather walk across broken glass than be here listening to this announcement. However, I want to ... '

This method alarms some inexperienced presenters. They argue that it will encourage dissent. In fact, it has the opposite effect because you're showing that you know 'where the audience is coming from'. Nothing is quite so effective for defusing trouble. Yes, you may trigger a small vocal outburst, but the overall effect is to deal with the trouble before it happens, or at least take a lot of the dynamite out of it. Which reminds me of the motto of the George clan: *Sic Ego Tibi,* which can be translated loosely as 'I'm going to do it to you before you do it to me'.

Now all that remains is to fill in your closing spotlight (see Figure 3.5). Lord Mancroft once said, 'A speech is like a love affair. Any fool can start it, but to end it requires considerable skill.' But it's easier than Mancroft thought, especially if you use more of the kind of material you put in the opening spotlight. It could be a call to action. It could be a quote. It could be both. For example, 'And finally, as Oscar Wilde put it: "When I was young I thought money was the most important thing in life; now I am old I know that it is." Now let's all go out there and get wealthy!'

Well, there are the four preparation steps: write the city-view, brainstorm, connect, organise. Now it's just a matter of delivering everything in the right order.

Figure 3.5
Enter your closing spotlight

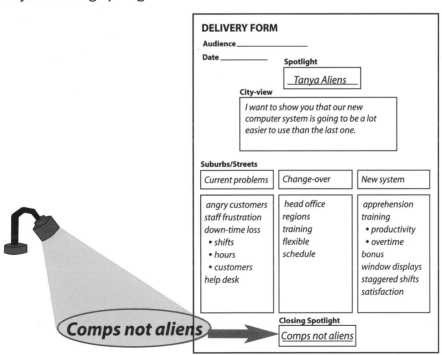

Rehearse the order of delivery

1. *Introduction:* spotlight city-view, suburbs preview.
2. *Main body:* suburb 1, suburb 2, suburb 3, etc.
3. *Conclusion:* suburbs review, city-view review, closing spotlight.

Tell them what you're going to tell them, tell them, then tell them what you told them: this old saying has been around for many decades and with good reason. It works. Audiences appreciate it and they understand the content better. Watch how the saying is put to work in the example below. Make it work for your own material.

INTRODUCTION (Telling them what you're going to tell them)

Rehearse your own introduction from your delivery form.

Opening spotlight ➔ (link)	'Afternoon everyone. Michelle Robbins tells me her worried three-year-old daughter Tanya found her in the garden last night and demanded to know if computers were for fighting aliens … which describes our situation, doesn't it? Most of us feel as if we're fighting an alien culture.'
City-view ➔	'This morning I want to show you that the new computer system is going to be much easier to use and much more efficient than the one we've had.'
Suburbs preview ➔ (formal presentations only. Very brief — with pauses between)	'We'll look at our current problems … [pause] … we'll look at the change-over timetable [pause] … and we'll look at what we can expect from the new system.'
Time and questions? ➔ (if necessary)	'We should be finished by lunch time … Do ask questions as we go …'

Once you get used to this system, you'll find you can deliver a stirring introduction with nothing more than five minutes notice and a few words scribbled on the delivery form.

MAIN BODY (Telling them)

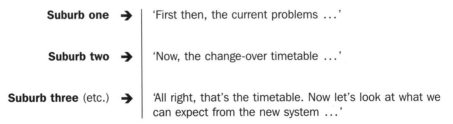

Suburb one ➔	'First then, the current problems …'
Suburb two ➔	'Now, the change-over timetable …'
Suburb three (etc.) ➔	'All right, that's the timetable. Now let's look at what we can expect from the new system …'

CONCLUSION (Telling them what you told them)

Suburbs review ➜ (formal presentations only)	'We've seen how disastrous the old system has been … [pause] we've seen we'll be in for a difficult change-over … [pause] … but we've also seen how much we've got to gain from the change.'
City-view review ➜	'So, I'm asking you to accept that the new system's not only going to increase our efficiency, it's going to transform working conditions for all of us.'
Closing spotlight ➜	'Young Tanya Robbins was probably relieved to discover that she didn't have to fight aliens. I hope we'll all feel the same relief when we install the new computer system. Thank you.'

DON'T WRITE PROMPT NOTES TO BE HAND-HELD

Hand-held prompt cards are very difficult to use naturally. For example there's no such thing as an unobtrusive glance at your cards. It's all too obvious and usually looks like an awkward compromise. Far better are prompt notes left on a nearby surface. The Delivery Form is ideal. When you need a reminder, you make an open movement to it, usually pausing to do so.

HOW DO I LAY OUT A FULLY WRITTEN SPEECH?

Just a minute, are you sure about this? As you've seen, the delivery form is mostly a bullet point abbreviated list, a compromise between two extremes: complete spontaneity and the fully written speech. If you read out a speech, you're settling for second best. That's because no matter how good your preparation and your knowledge of the people expected to attend, it can never be good enough to predict every nuance of interaction between you and a real audience.

But sometimes there's no choice. You're lumbered with someone else's speech, or tight legal issues make spontaneity risky, or perhaps the audience is going to be jammed with critics, pens and solicitors poised, waiting for the slightest slip. If you must write every word in advance, follow these pointers.

On each page:
- Use a large, easy-to-read font.
- Make every sentence a separate paragraph and don't break any sentence with a page change.
- Use 1.5 line-spacing with an extra line before the paragraph. Indent each first line.
- Put page numbers in every corner. Dropping your notes then taking too long to sort them out can make for a comedy act with you as the main attraction.

Here's a compromise layout if you want to allow for spontaneity, but you're determined not to abandon the security of a fully written speech:

- Read so that you don't seem to be reading.
- Take half a step back so that your eyes don't have to drop too much to look at your notes.
- Scan the first phrase of the sentence in silence, then look up.
- Engage the eyes of the audience and speak the first phrase.
- Look down as you read out the middle section of the sentence and scan ahead to the last phrase.
- Look up and engage the audience to speak the last phrase.
- Repeat for next sentence.

Use the guide that appears in Figure 3.6.

FIGURE 3.6
How to read and maintain eye contact

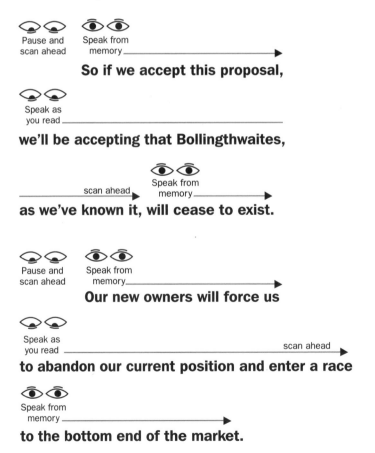

With practice, you'll look as if your attention is more on people than on paper. Most of us need practice because the method reverses our normal impulse (from fear of silence) to start uttering the words as soon as we start reading the beginning of the sentence. Make sure that each time you begin a new sentence you fully engage with the audience before you speak.

HOW TO PREPARE FOR A DIFFICULT OR CHALLENGING AUDIENCE

The good news is that it's no different from what you have just been practising. But you'll want to spend more time on some parts of the method. Pay special attention to:

- *Acknowledging the audience mood, feeling, or major objection.* Your tough audience will not listen to your facts until they hear you acknowledge their feelings and concerns. And remember — that does not mean agreeing with their argument or facts.
- *The city-view.* This is the core of your introduction. Give careful attention to telling the audience directly and openly what you want to achieve with them. The more difficult the audience, the more important this is. Openly telling them what you want to achieve with a difficult audience pays handsome dividends in terms of their respect for you. The opposite is true of presenters who reason that for a difficult audience it's better to skirt around the point. Audiences are very efficient x-ray machines. They also reserve a special place in hell for presenters who try to deceive them.
- *Pre-empting their objections, concerns and related questions.* Take it to them before they take it to you. This removes a great deal of audience steam.
- *Broadcasting on WIIFM.* The audience will feel that you are connected to them, not just speaking at them.

■ THE LAST-MINUTE CHECKLIST

You should have covered this one in the brainstorm, but it might be worth last-minute thought.

MENTALLY PREPARE FOR THE CRITICS

Anticipate the difficult questions and prepare just the essence of the answers. They should be pro-active answers, never defensive. For example:

Question: 'These budget cuts you've recommended, yours looks much smaller than ours.'

Answer: 'You'll see that I've not been even-handed with any of you. And that's a deliberate step — different departments should wear the pain differently.'

REHEARSE

Winston Churchill's valet was passing his bathroom one night, when he heard the sound of Churchill's voice above the sound of splashing in the bathtub.

'Were you speaking to me, Sir?' the valet called out.

'No,' Churchill snapped, annoyed at the interruption, 'I was addressing the House of Commons.'

Whatever rehearsal method you use, try to do your first one the day before and do it as close as you can to going to sleep. At night the subconscious goes to work on such adrenaline producing problems and draws on resources you didn't even know you had. Rehearse again in the morning and you'll find a marked improvement.

Act it, don't just say it. Act with all the enthusiasm and emphasis you can muster, because that registers it on your mind with attitude, which makes it ten times more likely to sink in.

- *Act it in front of a mirror.* Try to persuade your reflected self.
- Pace around in a room, talking to your imagined audience.
- *Enlist the help of a friend or colleague as a trial audience.* Again, treat it as a performance, not just rehearsal of verbal content. It's the most difficult method, but can be the most productive.
- *Rehearse to trees.* Don't knock it until you've tried it. Trees make a much better audience than an empty room at home. And if there's a stiff breeze, the applause is so convincing!

DRESS FOR THE PART

I once heard a speech entirely ruined by the clothes of the presenter. I remember this one in particular because at first sight there wasn't much difference between his clothes and ours. Most of us were in good jeans, open necked shirts and casual shoes. He was in old jeans held up with string, a tee-shirt, and thongs, in each case only one grade down on what we wore. And yet the focus of the audience was so drawn to his attire, his message was lost. His intention, I guessed, was to say to his audience, 'I am not a stuffed shirt like those who normally give speeches'. At the intellectual level, they got that message. But at the visceral level they got entirely another, which said, 'I do not respect you'.

Consciously or subconsciously the audience demands that you respect them. You convey much of your respect, or lack of it, in the care you take with how you dress.

If possible, dress the same or slightly better than your audience, but never below your normal range.

That last part is there because you should never dress so far below your normal standard that it's just not you. You'll feel false, and your audience won't appreciate it. I once did a television feature on a bikie gang. Had I dressed the same or slightly better than the bikies I would have been seen as false or condescending and earned their contempt. I stayed in jacket and tie. They stayed in filthy jeans and tee-shirts. We got on fine. Some extra points:

- *Comfort*. Make sure the clothing is easy to wear.
- *Colour*. Wear something with a bright colour or two so the audience's eyes can stay on you more easily. For men in suits, the only option is a bright tie.
- *Pockets*. Bulging pockets are a distraction for the audience.
- *Shoes*. If the shoes can be shined, shine them. Under every stone, you'll find consultants with opinions on what you should wear in business. The only point they all agree on is that shoes that *can* shine *must*.
- *Hair*. Keep hair off the forehead, upper cheeks and lips. The visual signals from the face have importance way disproportionate to those from the rest of the body.

Women need to be especially careful. In spite of the march of gender equality, men can get away with poor dress sense and still be listened to. Women cannot. And the most demanding audience for a poorly dressed woman is women.

PUT DUTCH COURAGE BACK IN THE BOTTLE

I have seen some notable exceptions, but very few. Usually Dutch courage works brilliantly in the mind of the presenter. Shakespeare said, 'Drink provokes the desire but it takes away the performance.' I doubt if he had public speaking in mind, but it applies just as well.

GOT YOUR NOTES?

Don't scoff, it's easily done.

ARRIVE EARLY

If you arrive right on show time, assuming everything will be okay, you're flirting with disaster. Depending on the venue, you may have a lot to do. If it's a big occasion, then you'll need to develop immediate rapport with organisers and technicians. I say rapport because the vibes of your presentation begin from that moment. Your relationship with the chairperson will have a subtle effect on the tone of voice they use to introduce you. And take particular care with the technician who, when it comes to wielding power over your presentation, is next-in-line to God.

CHECK THE LAYOUT OF THE ROOM

There are some essential checks to do on the venue:
- *Is the promised equipment there?* Are all the visual aids in place? Immediately check every detail down to coloured felt pens. Making changes can be time-consuming.
- *Are the visual aids in the best location?* For example, you'll find it very difficult to have them directly behind you.
- *Is the audience going to be comfortable?* Does the air conditioning need turning up or down? Will they be able to see? Will they have sun shining directly on them?

- *Is the seating arrangement correct?* The best all-purpose arrangement is called the 'chevron' after a Non Commissioned Officer's stripes: rows angled about 20 degrees so everyone faces slightly inwards. For small formal groups needing to work with paper, my favourite is the plain boardroom style.

CHECK THAT EVERYTHING WORKS AND THAT YOU CAN WORK EVERYTHING

Never take it for granted that your equipment will work:

- Make sure you know which buttons to push. The audience will forgive only so much bumbling about trying to figure out how things work. Make sure machinery is ready to go, even down to getting the overhead projector pre-focused.
- If you have highly sequential visual aids, then you must have them in precisely the right order. If you're dependent on someone else to cue the computer display, or slide change, then go over the cues with that person.
- If you have sound effects, make sure that they're at the right level. If it's background, then the right level is just below what is consciously noticed while you're speaking.
- For big venues, check the lighting to be directed at you. Best is two lights, 45 degrees to each side of centre and 45 degrees up from the horizontal. And remember that even if you can't see your audience, they need to see you well-lit. Walking in and out of the pool of light will have the same effect as switching your audience on and off.

GIVE SPECIAL ATTENTION TO MICROPHONE AND LECTERN

These can either polish your halo or destroy you.

- *Is the lectern too high?* If it's above your sternum, it is, and you may need to find a box. Ruth Richardson, a prominent but very short cabinet minister, used to carry a box to the lectern, step up onto it and give impressive, authoritative speeches.
- *Can the microphone be moved from the lectern?* If it can be, find out how. If it can't, then you've got a choice: either stay behind the lectern or forget both lectern and microphone. For smaller audiences, I would certainly do without both.
- *Check how to speak into the microphone.* Each microphone type has its own personality. Does it rub on your jacket when you move? Can you turn your head and still be heard?
- *Is the microphone at the right sound level?* Check with the technician.

The microphone is at the right level and distance when you don't need to shout yet you still have to project.

- *The audience doesn't just have to hear you clearly, it has to see you projecting to them.* It's an odd, distracting sensation to sit in an audience, hearing words but seeing the presenter making no effort to reach you.

- *What kind of microphone?* Lapel mikes are the most popular, because you have freedom to move and you can turn your head and still be heard easily. A radio microphone gives you the greatest freedom, though it can be unreliable. A hand-microphone on a long cord is usually reliable, but — unless you're very practised — it will lag behind your head movements, weakening the sound. And if you don't move round with care, you become a walking spindle, providing light relief at the wrong time.

CHECK HOW YOU'RE GOING TO BE INTRODUCED

Beware of inappropriate introductions. Who wants a fanfare of your virtues and accomplishments when you're about to announce the closing of the factory.

TUNE INTO THE AUDIENCE AS THEY ARRIVE

When the audience starts arriving, your presentation is under way. Meet some individually. It's one of the best ways of overcoming pre-performance nerves, because knowing and recognising a few individuals transforms that frightening organism called an audience into a collection of real people. When you talk to the arriving individuals:

Shake them by the hand

The Romans are credited with inventing the handshake as a way of showing they were not armed. They shook them all the way up to the elbow, which may be over-enthusiastic on your part. In fact, hand shaking is a subtle art. The general rule is: a reasonably firm grip and a shake that lasts no more than three pumps, but easy on the vigour if it's between a man and a woman. It's well worth checking out your handshake with someone you trust to give you honest feedback. You may get a surprise.

Remember and use their names

The sweetest of sounds is our own name, because our name defines us. Each time someone uses it, we are painted more vividly into our own landscape. We can't help but respond positively to someone who makes the effort to do that. Here are two methods for remembering. Remember that the more you can work each method towards a feeling or an emotion, the better your memory will be. (Don't shy away from an emotion that is total fiction — it's just a memory trigger.)

- *Method 1 — A rhyming word.* A nonsense rhyme works, but it's better if the word has meaning.
  'Hi, I'm Polly.'
  'Daniel.' [Polly. Molly, good golly Miss Molly. Good golly! Polly!]
  'Good morning, Simon. I'm Hillary Turner.'
  'Ah, good morning Hillary.' Hillary Turner. [Hillary, Sillary, Celery Turner, burner hot ouch. Ouch! Hillary Turner!]

- *Method 2 — Association*. Find something to associate with the name, possibly from the person's body, body language or clothes.

> 'How d'you do. Trevor Hill's the name.'
> 'Hi. I'm Sue.' [Trevor. Cardigan. Red. Bed. Fed. FBI agent Trevor Hill!]
> 'Hello, I've been trying get hold of you all evening. I'm Brian Barton.'
> 'Pleased to meet you.' [Brian. Same Christian name as my wealthy cousin. Brian. Rich Brian Barton!]

Listen to them

I mean really listen. Eleventh-hour contact like this will alert you to audience mood, feeling or opinion that you have missed. Many individuals will fall all over themselves to let you glimpse their attitude to the forthcoming presentation. Vital stuff. Second, when you develop rapport with an individual, you lay the foundations of a subtle rapport with the entire audience.

LISTEN TO OTHER SPEAKERS

How are the other speakers interacting with the audience? What mood is the audience showing them? The answers will make subtle, appropriate differences to your style without you even trying.

Besides, you can almost always count on a previous speaker to give you something to bounce off. For example: you take the floor, look sadly at the previous speaker and say, 'I'm sorry Frank, I think you've got it all wrong with that tree hut. We built ours so that we can move in when the children drive us insane'. Rapport, even before you begin the first prepared word. Good debaters always listen to each other, looking for ammunition.

REHEARSE SPOTLIGHT, CITY-VIEW AND SUBURB HEADINGS

The first few sentences are usually the hardest. So, mentally rehearse the opening ideas, though not every word or you'll sound stiff. If you can, avoid the prompt notes at the beginning. It looks less than convincing to need a piece of paper to tell you when to say 'Welcome' or 'Thank you' or 'Good morning'. And it's even more unconvincing to do the same thing in the middle of a city-view. 'Today I'm going to convince you that … (hesitation, looking at paper) … our strategic plan is a matter of life and death.'

FINAL TIPS FOR HANDLING PRE-PERFORMANCE NERVES

You understand that nervous energy is a friend, but you still have the sweaty palms, dry mouth and bronco heart? Join a large club. And it certainly pays to rid yourself of the excess symptoms. Try these tips:

- *Remind yourself of your performance key*. It will help put your nervous energy to work for you.

- *Use a relaxation or 'grounding' exercise.* Do Activity 9 (Chapter 7, page 123) — it's the most successful I know and the only one I now use. Do it quietly or you'll give the wrong message to anyone of the right gender.
- *Drink only lukewarm liquids.* Iced drinks will put your larynx into the Antarctic which is not a region known for producing great opera singers. Don't drink carbonated liquids unless you want to belch unintentionally and spectacularly into the microphone.

■ GETTING THE MOST OUT OF AUDIOVISUAL AIDS

'I urge you to incorporate all the visual aids you can to support, but not make, your main arguments,' Tom Hopkins, *How to Master the Art of Selling*

Are you in control of your audiovisual aids, or are they in control of you? In this age of seductive programs like PowerPoint, are you their master? Or have you become their slave, relieved that you can divert audience attention away from you? If it's the second, then those aids are not building your authority — they're undermining it.

One thing is certain. People are more convinced by people than by machines. The connection, control and rhythm you establish between you, your audience and the visual aids might be more important to your impact than the content of the aids. General rules are difficult because many people have differing opinions on what irritates or impresses them about audiovisual aids. Even so, what follows is designed to give you control of aids so that they build your authority and the impact of your message.

PREPARING AUDIOVISUAL AIDS
Much of how smoothly you are able to use and capitalise on your audiovisual aids is in the preparation. Don't skimp here.

Content
Decide on your main points, then design visual aids to support them — not the other way around. Be careful that you don't simply write out your main points in full on the screen, expecting the audience to absorb them while you read them out. Bullet-point text should be very sparingly used — leaving you the option to expand verbally.

Make them relevant
Make each aid relevant to that audience. Ask yourself what main impression your audience will get. If it's not the impression you want, leave it out.

Keep them simple

Simple and uncluttered. A visual display is seen as a whole, but most audiences can only absorb one idea at a time. Make sure it contains only the information related to your message. For example, if you make a bar graph to show social club spending this year compared with last, you only need the title, two bars, two years, and the two amounts. Overnumbering each graph axis, putting in surplus information and bright colours that don't highlight the point all undermine your message. Company logos are acceptable as long as they're simple and unobtrusive.

Resist every temptation to throw up a table of figures then say to the audience, 'I just want to show you this number down here; yes here it is: 13th row, 5th from the right.'

But do add relevant visual interest

Figures on a graphic are often so dry they have little impact on the audience. For example, divorces in 1976: 684. Increase in a year: 9.5 per cent. Got the emotional impact? Of course not. So in your graphic you need to add relevant visual interest, preferably relevant human interest:

- *Add a picture*. It could be a drawing of an object, a cartoon, even a photograph. If the picture can highlight an emotion, so much the better. For example, a picture of a couple back-to-back, the space between them for your numbers on divorces.
- *Make your message out of pictures*. For example, a graph of the rise in spending on armaments might only register as a sloping line to your audience. But what if that line were the barrel of a Scorpion tank? Or you might run a retail flower company and want a chart that compares sales of the different varieties of flowers for weddings. Imagine a bunch of the very flowers you're talking about, each variety in proportion and with a percentage number above it.

Make numbers fit the audience

Every digit in the figure 9.75 per cent might be relevant to bankers dissecting interest rates. But if you're telling parents about the proportion of youngsters who have accidents leading to injury, the number should be 10 per cent, or 1 in 10.

Make printing large

The simpler the aid, the easier it is to see. For transparencies, lay the result at your feet and stand up. If you can't read the words, the font is too small.

Pre-exposure of lists: show the whole, then the part

If there was a top ten of audience irritants, it would have to include presenters who reveal lists point by point without showing the whole list first. Audiences feel manipulated. And they don't follow logical development of a list without the visual reference point of the whole. Show them the whole list, then use a pointer on individual items, or — if you must — cover and reveal.

Software programs like PowerPoint carry the tools for an excellent antidote to the problem. Show the list first on the screen at reduced intensity, then, without ever losing sight of the list, highlight and talk about each item in turn, ending with all items highlighted.

FIGURE 3.7
Exposing lists of items

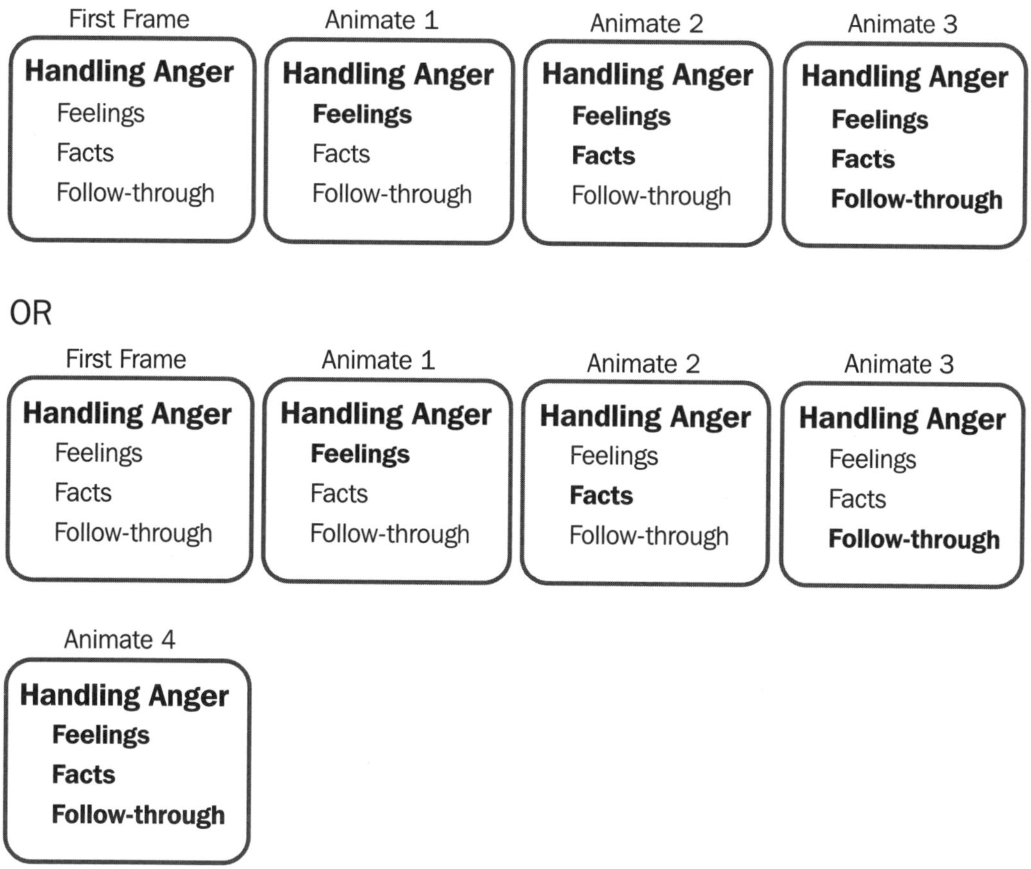

First Frame	Animate 1	Animate 2	Animate 3
Handling Anger Feelings Facts Follow-through	**Handling Anger** **Feelings** Facts Follow-through	**Handling Anger** **Feelings** **Facts** Follow-through	**Handling Anger** **Feelings** **Facts** **Follow-through**

OR

First Frame	Animate 1	Animate 2	Animate 3
Handling Anger Feelings Facts Follow-through	**Handling Anger** **Feelings** Facts Follow-through	**Handling Anger** Feelings **Facts** Follow-through	**Handling Anger** Feelings Facts **Follow-through**

Animate 4

Handling Anger
Feelings
Facts
Follow-through

However, keep in mind that some are irritated by anything other than being shown the whole list, without changes, immediately. If you're going to cater to that feeling, then you'll need to verbally highlight which point you're talking about to avoid that other irritation, *Where are we? What's she referring to?*

■ USING VISUAL AIDS EFFECTIVELY

Next time you see a good presenter using visual aids, watch for the rhythm — a coordinated rhythm of visual change, body movement, silence and talking. Here's how to start.

THE CORE PRINCIPLE

Being of sound mind, you speak to people, not objects. For this part, think of using a whiteboard, or referring to your speech notes.

The order is talk, then turn and touch or point (be silent), then turn and talk again. Let's walk through it:

1. Talk only while you have eye contact with the audience. Practise beginning to turn your body to the whiteboard while your head and eyes stay on the audience for the last words. Don't send the last words to the wall or window on the way around.

2. Stay silent while you write (or point or look), and while you turn your head back towards the audience.

3. Start talking only when you have re-established eye contact with the audience (not when you are merely looking in their direction). Practise turning your head and eyes quickly back to the audience, ahead of your body.

The exception

You can talk and look at a screen or whiteboard simultaneously, but only if you use your body language to indicate that you are (in part) one of the audience. To do so, take a step or two towards the audience and to the side, then turn to look at the screen with them. Now they'll accept you talking to the screen, as long as you also turn to them regularly. However, as soon as you stride up to the screen with your hand or a pointer, you have given away that right to talk while looking at objects and you need to return to the core principle. A little rehearsal will show you that there is a zone in between the two positions in which you can move, but not stand still. Move quickly, assertively — be definitely in one position or the other.

You can also talk while looking at your paperwork, but only if the audience is also looking at their own copies of the same thing.

Avoiding 'this is a cow'

Experienced broadcasters will often use this phrase to criticise a rookie reporter's item. It says that the reporter is telling people what they can see perfectly well for themselves — implying that they are stupid. The same is true of rookie presenters who show a slide or transparency, then read out the exact words on the screen, or (worse), tell you what you're looking at visually. The phrase 'show and tell' is often used in the same way. In fact, reversing that is the best general rule for avoiding the mistake.

Tell, then show, then tell what they can't see for themselves.

FIGURE 3.8
Avoiding 'this is a cow'

Show

Tell

'Here's a cow and this is a diagram of the stomachs, showing the ruminant digestive system with four chambers.'

Show

Tell

'We could expand our diet if we had a rather more complex digestive system.'

(pause) **Tell what they can't see:**
'If Daisy didn't have more than one stomach, she wouldn't be able to digest grass. The first of these four chambers is ...'

When you want text in bullet points, you must still avoid reading out word for word. Figure 3.9 shows what to do when you want full sentences on screen:

FIGURE 3.9
Using bullet points

Show

Ruminants

- Ruminants are cud-chewing, cloven-hoofed animals.
- The ruminant digestive system involves four stomach chambers.

Tell

'We could expand our diet if we had a rather more complex digestive system.'

(pause) *Tell what they can't see:*
'The first point ... other ruminants? Sheep, goats, deer, and giraffes.'

(pause)
'Second point ... two of those chambers are for fermenting or pre-digestion ... that's what leads to the cud-chewing ...'

And — usually the best — when you want short summary phrases on screen (as per Figure 3.10):

FIGURE 3.10
Using short summary phrases

Show

Ruminants

- Cud-chewing, cloven-hoofed
- Four stomach chambers.

Tell

'We could expand our diet if we had a rather more complex digestive system.'

(pause) *Tell what they can't see:*
'First point ... Not just the cow ... sheep, goats, deer, giraffes.'

(pause)
'Second point ... Two chambers are for pre-digestion fermenting, then up to the mouth for more chewing, then back to the next two chambers for the finishing touches.'

Unfortunately, we can't make a blanket rule of not reading screen words. A quote, for example, works better if you do read it out, so does an especially important set of words. A general rule is dangerous, but for a rough guide try this: you can read the words out word for word if you can imbue them with passion. And even then you might need the audience's permission. For example, 'This is important. Let me read it out ...' or 'I love this. Let me read it out ...'

The pause: an aid to your aids

If you want to cripple the effectiveness of your visual aid, keep firing words at the audience when they first see it. But if you want a full, healthy impact, stop talking. A pause for as little as two seconds can make a dramatic difference.

Pause with each visual change, so your audience has time to take it in.

When you go to change an overhead transparency:
- stop talking
- move to the projector in silence (your body announces the forthcoming change). Stay silent to allow the visual change to sink in
- re-establish eye contact with the audience from beside the projector and speak again, *or* move back to be with the audience, turn to the screen and speak again.

When you're about to press the button to make a visual change, use your body language to announce the change:
- stop talking
- turn to the screen (your body is announcing a change — especially important when it's a small change). Press the button to make the change. Pause for at least one second, looking at the screen with the audience
- speak again.

A caution

You are the show — not your visual aids.

Remember that your visual aids are just aids — they should seldom be the main act. Aids can strongly improve your impact, but in the end, people respond best to people. Modern technology has turned us all into wizards, able to manipulate squillabytes of words and graphics at the wave of the electronic wand. That's irresistible to many presenters. We've all seen audiovisual spectaculars whose unstated message is, 'Haven't I turned on a great audiovisual spectacle'. Actually it might be breathtaking, but when we get the lungs going again there's a nagging question: 'What was it about? What was the point?' Then we ask our neighbours, 'Who was that presenter, anyway? Can you remember their name?'

You are the best visual aid you have. In fact, one research finding says that if you use a visual aid to make your first point, you increase the retention rate from 15 to 40 per cent. But with each additional visual aid that rate increase is much smaller. If they dominate your presentation, the retention rate will plummet. Most audiences are not swayed to action by facts, figures or light and sound technology, but by a real person.

Now that we've put visual aids in their place as subordinates, let's use them, and use them well. They are a potent tool.

Beware the over-use of whizz-bang electronic visuals

When PowerPoint arrived, many presenters fell upon it with huge gratitude, saying, 'Now I too can look great!' They have made the words and letters zip and zap and beep and buzz until our ears curl, teeth rattle and eyeballs roll in their sockets. Now, wherever I go, I find people who tell me they get annoyed with presenters who over-use the whizz-bang visual tools.

Here's a good general rule. Think of each electronic tool as being like putting a word in capital letters. Would you write anyone a letter with every second word in caps? If so, you may well be reading this from the secure unit of a psychiatric institution. Keep taking the pills.

Recently the U.S. Chairman of Joint Chiefs of Staff — fed up with over-use of fancy audio-visuals — issued an order down through the ranks at the Pentagon: get to the point!

chapter 4

Boosting your impact on the audience

- Establishing audience rapport

- Recovering from mistakes

- Using silence, body language and humour

'Take 'em by surprise.' Barbara Castle, British MP

The best impact on an audience comes from achieving 'flow'. But there are many other effective ways of increasing your influence on your audience.

■ GIVE THE GREETING LIFE

How often we hear the opposite. The speaker opens in a tone that is flatter than a funeral march: 'I would like to take this opportunity to express my thanks for the opportunity . . . '

Thanks? With a monotone? No way. No-one who means it says it like that.

'. . . to speak to you today and to say what a pleasure it is . . . '

Pleasure? In a dull monotone?

Confronted with this apparent insincerity, the audience decides before the end of the sentence that this is not going to be a pleasure for them. We don't do that to real people, so why do it to an audience? If you don't feel grateful, don't say thank you. If you don't feel pleasure, don't say you do. But if you can or do feel either, say so with the feeling. With life! Say it like you mean it!

■ HOW CAN I BUILD RAPPORT RIGHT AT THE BEGINNING?

The moment the speaker interacts with the audience, the initial awkwardness and tensions go. The whole energy of the performance lifts, genuine warmth comes into the speaker's eyes and they are instantly more natural. Some speakers are deathly afraid of audience interaction and ask their audiences to hold questions to the end, not realising what a gift they're throwing away. But the same people are converts once they've tried deliberate interaction. Some suggestions:

Smaller audiences	
Use someone's name.	'I shouldn't tell you this. Dale will have it in the company newsletter before the tea break.'
Ask an open ended question.	'I know some of you have avoided taking on new staff so far. Why is that?'
Larger audiences	
Ask a question and comment on the answer.	'How many of you came here expecting a solution? Okay, well in your shoes I would too, but it's not going to happen because . . . '

If your purpose is to establish rapport, ask a question and wait for the answer.
If necessary, ask for the answer again either directly or as a show of hands.

■ SIGNPOST YOUR PRESENTATION

Some entertainers are so accomplished that the audience will luxuriate in the detail, suspending their desire to know where they are. But if it's not pure entertainment, then no matter how good you are, your presentation needs signposting.

> **Audience insatiable desire no. 1: 'At all times I want to know where I am in your presentation'.**

Some examples of typical signposting phrases:
'Now, the sales figures.'
'That's enough on the nature of arachnophobia ... let's get onto how we overcome it.'
'As you'll see later ...'
'Remember I told you that ... Well, here's the pay-off ...'
'And that's not the only cause of death in indoor plants ...'

■ HOW CAN I GIVE THEM VARIETY?

This is more important than having a good energy level. Some public speakers are so energised that you expect them to do handstands and scorch the walls. For the first few minutes, the speaker might have you riveted. But if they stay a ball of fire you will still power down your message receptors and your last conscious thought might be a vain hope that someone will bring in a hose to put them out.

> **Audience insatiable desire no. 2: 'Give me variety'.**

The audience is looking for changes in all of the eight components that make up your energy level: speed, tone, pitch, volume, intensity, body language, emphasis, silence. It's no good trying to remember a list like that, but you don't need to if you develop a 'surprise them' frame of mind. Car passengers can sleep on a smooth or a rough road as long as the smoothness or roughness is constant. They can't sleep if the ride is unpredictable.

Here are a few tips. They're better rehearsed first, with a friend or colleague who can give you honest feedback. Ask that person to sit a few feet away and impersonate an audience of twenty.

You may wonder how a story-telling demeanour can be useful for a serious, work-related topic. Some workshop trainees have had serious doubts. But when they try it — certain that they'll look stupid — they're surprised to find their colleagues delighted at the improvement. Try it yourself. You'll never look back.

- Use *emphasis* to vary pace. When you come to a point you want to emphasise, help the emphasis by changing pace, usually slowing down.

'He parked his shiny new truck across my driveway and he left it there ... all ... day!'

- Start building in and enjoying *pauses*.

- Use your *full range of tone*. Show your friend or colleague this picture and ask if you squashed your tonal range.

- *Read a story to a child*, giving full poetic licence to the performance. Enjoy making the 'ups' very high and the 'lows' very low.
- Use your *eyebrows* to lift your tone when you want emphasis.
- Use your *gestures* to tell part of the story to a child. Use your whole body. Jump up and act out some parts.
- *Change intensity*. Just as a pause can be powerful, so can a stage whisper. Choose an appropriate important part of your speech. Practise a sudden dropping of the voice, slowing down, putting tension into eyes and gestures.

'On top of that he had the nerve ... *(pause, look from one part of the audience to another)* ... to criticise the message we wrote on the side of his truck.'

'Why grandma ... what big ears you have!' *(eyebrows up on grandma and up on ears).'*

■ WHAT DO I DO WHEN I MAKE AN EMBARRASSING MISTAKE?

The trick is to realise that it's almost never the mistake that destroys you, rather it's your embarrassment. Audiences forgive mistakes quickly. They don't easily forgive or forget embarrassment. Mistakes can be made by anyone, but embarrassment is a sign of weakness.

The answer is almost stupidly obvious: a variation on Life Choice No. 1: choose your attitude to any circumstance.

Choose to be unembarrassable.

Put it another way: it's not what happens, it's how you handle what happens.

My father told me of an incident on an Egyptian beach in the Second World War. The battalion was on R & R, with soldiers on the beach. Local Egyptians were there also, including a young, rather aristocratic-looking woman. She was knocked down by an unexpectedly big wave, which neatly removed her upper clothing. Now what would you expect from soldiers on R & R. Cat calls? Jeering? Whistles? No. The woman stood, retrieved her clothing and donned it with such poise and dignity that every soldier stood and applauded as she left the beach.

Embarrassment works like fear. If you don't feel embarrassed, there is nothing to be embarrassed about. Most audiences want you to be unembarrassable.

Here's how to do it:

- Be open with the audience about what's happening. If that means admitting a mistake, do so matter-of-factly, knowing that in the long view there is much, much more to you than an error.
- Laugh *with* the audience at yourself. This is especially suitable for trivial mistakes. When something goes wrong:

Share their enjoyment!

- After a pause for the merriment to die down, *resume your original demeanour.*

A manager farewelled an old colleague in front of 200 wharfies, a deeply cynical and formidable audience, easily capable of humiliating any 'stuffed-shirt' management presenter. Even though that colleague had been a personal friend for decades, he forgot his name at the crucial moment. So he turned with a calm smile to the wharfies and said, 'You know, I've known this guy for 25 years and do you think I can remember his name?' The wharfies roared with laughter, laughing with him. Imagine if he had stuttered and stammered and tried to cover up!

Visualise this scenario. You have just dropped your carefully ordered transparencies in mid-speech. They're all over the floor. Now try these two ways of handling the problem.

First, the worst. You scoop them up awkwardly, and sort them with a mumbled, flustered apology. The audience feels your embarrassment as acutely as if you were injecting them with a poison. It responds with pity, then irritation and, in the worst cases of embarrassment, contempt. Your clumsiness with the overheads will be remembered!

But now the alternative. You look down at the transparencies, spread your arms then roll your eyeballs as if to say, *Wouldn't you know it, the last thing a presenter needs!* (Being open with the audience.) There's a ripple of laughter. You scoop the transparencies up. With a look of amusement in your eyes (laughing with the audience at yourself) you say firmly to the audience, 'One moment', you get the transparencies back in order, then continue. Now your clumsiness with the overheads is swiftly forgotten! It's the kind of accident-handling or mistake-handling that makes audiences admire you and would-be presenters envy your poise and presence.

Incidentally, choosing to be unembarrassable does not mean that you shouldn't apologise for anything. Sometimes you must apologise to an audience as a matter of honour, but do so firmly, assertively, and without embarrassment.

■ BE OPEN, BUT NOT AN OPEN BOOK

I'm not talking about telling the truth or lying. In the long run it's suicidal to mislead an audience. Politicians are very slow learners on that point. Somehow, someone always knows and is willing to spread the word. By openness I'm talking about acknowledging everything that's happening, at the factual level and the emotional level.

- *Acknowledge opposition.* If your argument is going to be opposed by others, acknowledge the opposing argument. If there's likely to be a feeling about your argument, acknowledge the feeling.
- *Don't pretend knowledge you don't have.* Consciously or subconsciously, you'll always be found out. Strange, but true. An audience that doesn't consciously decide you're faking it will feel uneasy about you. Audiences know.
- *Do admit your mistakes.* Never with embarrassment or humility, always with matter-of-fact acknowledgment. You are bigger than your mistakes.

However, make sure you are only open on subjects that flow naturally out of the topic or the needs of the audience that day. If you're keen to be liked by an audience, it's tempting to reveal unrelated personal details about yourself. That will come across as naïve or ingratiating.

■ WHAT DO I DO WHEN MY PERSONAL VIEWS CONFLICT WITH WHAT I'M PRESENTING?

The answer depends on whether you are talking to an internal or external audience.

THE MANAGER AND THE INTERNAL AUDIENCE

Let's say your job is to get the despatch and delivery staff in behind the new trucking schedule, which, in theory, is going to reduce costs and raise profits. Personally, you think the new schedule is a disaster. You made your feelings plain in the planning, but you were overruled.

In the middle of your presentation, one of the delivery staff asks, 'Yes, but what's your personal view, John? Isn't this going to backfire?'

There's the dilemma. The mental dialogue is *If I'm honest I betray the company paying me to represent them. If I lie, I betray myself and my staff.* The most immediate temptation is probably the bare-faced lie, 'Yes, I think it'll work.' But that will do no more than announce the funeral of your personal credibility, and it deserves words from the managing director about misguided loyalty. Let's leave that one behind us. Here's a more tempting answer. 'I wouldn't tell you that one way or the other, because I'm not here to give my personal view.' But that won't work either, because to the staff you can't be simply a title and a non-person. They won't accept it as anything but a cover up and they'll be uneasy.

The key to the answer is the audience — it's the staff you're talking to. They, too, are the company and a company that lies to itself is sick. Honesty to staff looks after the company's health and has to be a greater priority than worries about expressing reservations. Here's the answer:

For an internal audience, be constructively honest about your own opinions.

You might use language like this: 'Personally, I've had reservations. But I was a lone voice on it and this policy has come out of days of weighing different arguments. Now that it's decided we need to do our part to make sure that it works and works well.' If questioned further about those reservations, take the attitude that they are now irrelevant. If any company is foolish enough to criticise you for that approach, look for a healthier company.

However, there's honesty, and then there's honesty delivered with a baseball bat. If any manager of mine were to answer, 'Well, now that you ask, I think it's a load of weasel droppings,' we would probably have a discussion about heads rolling.

THE MANAGER AND THE EXTERNAL AUDIENCE

Now we have to draw a line between honesty and revealing personal opinions. When you represent your organisation externally, you owe strangers honesty *but you don't owe them personal disclosures.* The line may be hard to draw, depending on to what extent you are in front of the external audience as yourself and to what extent as a manager. If you're there predominantly because you represent your organisation, then here's the rule:

For an external audience, be constructively honest without revealing your personal opinions.

Now, the sentence we tried and rejected above, has a chance of working. Say it lightly and dismissively: 'Oh no, I wouldn't tell you that one way or the other, because I'm here to represent my company, not to give my personal view.' It works only if the company hat is the only one on your head. And even then it only works up to a point. In spite of the phrase 'one way or the other', it may still sound like a face-saver. Your tone will carry it as long as it implies *Good grief no, it would be most inappropriate to give my personal opinion when I'm here representing my company*. In fact, in some situations, that sentence might work said out loud.

■ KEEP YOUR BODY LANGUAGE OPEN

When you use your performance key to unlock an excellent performance, you'll keep your stance open without even thinking about it. When you perform well, you're using a style that implies, *I am happy to be seen, known and understood by you*. Your body language expresses that same thing.

Do:

- adopt a 'home' position or stance. That's a position you decide on in advance that looks comfortable and is comfortable. It works particularly well if you're suddenly stricken with being over-conscious of your body language. Return to it until you feel comfortable again and no one need know. If you're standing, the home position should be not be symmetric — that is not exactly the same on both sides of a line down the centre of your body. Just putting your weight on one leg can do it.
- adopt gestures that take your arms away from your body. However, take care with international audiences. The first man on the moon, Neil Armstrong, closed thumb and index finger and sent the televised gesture earthwards. He meant 'everything's okay', but millions in the Eastern Block thought he was describing them as the south end of the alimentary canal. In a parade, former U.S. First Lady Barbara Bush held up an index and little finger, the recognition signal for Texas University. In Italy, they took the gesture to mean that she was cuckolding her husband and that the entire University Brass Band (who were returning the signal) were helping her do so.

Don't:

- allow your hands to join constantly, either in front or behind. Hand-wringing or hand-washing movements are definitely wrong
- adopt any symmetric posture for too long.

For informal occasions, here's a useful trick. Start with one hand, or just a thumb, in a trouser pocket. Use the other hand for emphasis, pulling out the first hand when you need it. Once you get into the flow, you'll find you don't need to return to the pocket. For people without pockets, try holding a small object like a pen to get you started, putting it down when you're under way. Don't click the pen!

■ SIT UP!

We've all seen variations on this movie scene: Sheriff Dylan Ozick Jr is in his office, relaxing, feet crossed and on the table, Budweiser at hand, six gallon hat pulled down over his forehead. The phone rings. Only his hand moves, lazily reaching for the receiver, just as lazily bringing it back to his ear.

'Yo,' he says in a bored voice.

We can't hear the voice at the other end, but whatever it says has a remarkable effect on Sheriff Dylan Ozick Jr. His eyes widen, his feet dive for the ground, he pulls his chair up to the desk, straightens his upper back and inclines slightly forward.

'Yes, Mr President,' he says.

Straightens his upper back and inclines slightly forward? Yes, because instinctively we know that we perform better with that posture when we're sitting. Many people override that instinct with the false belief that we do better when we're relaxed. We don't. Eighty per cent of our air normally comes from full operation of the diaphragm. If we don't have a straight upper back, we can't operate the diaphragm properly and have little access to that eighty per cent.

■ THE POWER OF SILENCE

Silence is one of the most powerful words in the English language. Beginners try desperately to fill silences, even while the audience's eyes glaze over at the monotony of sound. Experienced speakers deliberately inject silences as part of an overall rhythm and flow that gives them power.

The longer you can pause, the more status your audience will subconsciously award you.

As he dismisses 3B, the maths teacher says, 'I want to see Timkins, Smythe and Carruthers. The rest of you may go.' Timkins, Smythe and Carruthers glance at each other fearfully and approach, wringing caps in hands and stand, white-faced, before him.

'Well, well, well,' he says and looks slowly from one pair of petrified eyes to the next. In silence.

Carruthers and Timkins swallow simultaneously. More silence.

'It wasn't my fault,' squeaks Timkins. 'They made me.'

The maths teacher breathes in and he breathes out.

'I didn't!' Carruthers blurts, 'He brought the matches. And Smythe lit it!'

A blatant case of interrogating children with injections of silence. And even if you don't want your audience to babble simultaneous confessions, never underestimate the power of silence for dramatic emphasis.

■ BIGGER AUDIENCES WANT YOU TO BE BIGGER

Yes, you as well as the visual aids. Not the physical size of your body, of course, but what you do with it.

- Exaggerate your gestures. Exaggerate your expressions, frown deeper, smile wider, raise eyebrows higher. Lengthen your movements from one side to the other.
- Increase average energy. Increase average volume. Make bigger fluctuations to your energy level. Increase the range of your voice. Go higher and lower. Make bigger changes to the speed of your words.
- Exaggerate moments of intensity. Make emphasis more emphatic.
- Lengthen your pauses. That's why you can go back to the lectern to look at your notes and return in silence.
- If you're using a microphone, project almost as much as if you had no amplification.

■ YOUR NOTES AND THE LECTERN

Keep your notes out of obvious sight as you move to the lectern. You don't have to look like James Bond's furtive cousin, but the audience doesn't appreciate your need for a prompt being waved in their faces.

Keep half a pace back from the lectern, so that when you drop your eyes to your notes, you don't have to drop your head.

If you have more than one page, slide the pages, don't turn them.

■ TERMINATE THE LECTERN TANGO

Imagine that you're two years old. A large stranger comes to the door asking for directions. And he looks at you! You abandon a startled Teddy in mid-air and vanish behind your mother's skirt. Then, taking a firm grip on your mother's thighs, you put your head around, wide-eyed to look at the stranger.

Why do you think so many speakers take a death grip on their lecterns? Some speakers need security so badly their knuckles go white, and even if they don't break off bits of lectern they physically rock it in different directions. That's the lectern tango. It must be sorely tempting for some in the audience to call out and ask if they can reserve the last dance.

Yes. It is better to come on out from behind. It's part of the openness we've talked about earlier. In fact, most people want to come on out but find it difficult to abandon the false security.

However, having ventured out, there's often a problem with referring back to notes left on the lectern. It's another version of talking to people, not paper. But, when I try to tell a trainee that the answer is the same, they will often look at me as if I'm Honest John unloading a used car. *You must be joking. If I stop talking, there will be an awful silence. How can the audience cope with silence while I go all the way back to the lectern, look at my notes and return?!*

Many trainees are convinced only when they see themselves do it on a video replay. To the audience it looks right. Here are the steps to leaving the comfort and safety of the lectern, and to going back for a prompt.

1. Don't come out until you know that you're on a comfortable roll with your words and can speak spontaneously for a minute or two.
2. Stop speaking while your eyes are still on the audience.
3. Break eye contact with the audience.
4. Walk back, get the prompt, start walking out again.
5. Make eye contact with the audience.
6. Speak.

The audience not only copes with such silence, they want it. They want that pause. And the bigger the audience, the bigger the pause they want and — remember — the more status they'll give you. But, like any movement, it mustn't become frequent and predictable. If you need a lot of prompting you had better bring your notes with you, or stay behind the lectern.

■ TELL STORIES AND BECOME A GOOD STORYTELLER

Example: A first aid instructor is trying to impress her students with the fact that rescuers are sometimes more likely to react to blood than the victims themselves. If she told the principle only it might be, 'You'll find sometimes that you'll react to blood more than the victim does. If you don't guard against it, you could endanger the lives of the people you're trying to help.'

But what if she started like this:

> *In 1931, early in the morning of December 14, an air ace called Douglas Bader cartwheeled his plane along the runway. When the wreckage came to a halt, Bader sat there in what was left of the cockpit, critically injured. Men rushed out from the clubhouse, including the steward who had the foresight to bring brandy.*
>
> *'Here you are, sir,' said the steward. 'Have a bit of this brandy.'*
>
> *'No, thanks very much,' said Douglas Bader. 'I don't drink.'*
>
> *The steward leaned over to urge him, saw the blood spurting, turned ashen, then stood back and drank the brandy himself.*
>
> *The point is this, you'll find sometimes that you'll react to blood more than the victim does . . .*

Which way is more effective? A rhetorical question, of course. And notice that it's not just relating the facts of the story, it's storytelling.

USE COLOURFUL COMPARISONS
Example: 'She sped around that dormitory faster than a moggie in a dog pound.'

GET PERSONAL — GIVE YOUR STORIES STARS
Example: 'On a sunny day in 1914, a young man called Rupert Turner put on his tweed jacket, polished his teeth, strolled down to the local strip club ...'

GET DETAILED, GET PARTICULAR
Example: Not, 'Harold was in a bad mood yesterday.' Instead, 'Yesterday morning, Harold wakes up. The first thing he sees is the cracked plaster. The first thing he thinks is that there's no food in the cupboard. And the first thing he tastes is what's left on his tongue from the night before.'

Persuasive people paint pictures with their words. Mario Cuomo, former Mayor of New York, is one of the world's better speakers. At a Democratic convention he laid a whip into the Republicans with this word-picture gem: 'The Republicans believe that the wagon train will not make it to the frontier, unless some of the old, some of the young, some of the weak, are left behind by the side of the road! The strong, they tell us, will inherit the land. We Democrats believe something else. We Democrats believe that we can make it all the way with the whole family intact!'

Here's one of the most effective uses of word-pictures I know. It's a true story. I'm telling it third hand, but I think you'll agree that its strength survives such distortions:

> *Some years back, an American man left his wife and children for another woman. He maintained contact with his family, but didn't seem to understand the distress and suffering they were going through. His small daughter set out to try to make him understand. She wrote him a picture painted with words.*
>
> *'Dear Dad. I had a dream about Mum and me and Tina. We was driving along the road in the car. Mum was driving pretty good with us kids sitting in the back. We was laughing and telling jokes and Mum was laughing too. Then a huge big truck came roaring out of a yard and hit us in the side. The car was totalled, but we weren't killed. We went to hospital for a long time. After that we didn't want to do anything much and we just stayed home. But then we came outside and started playing again okay and we started playing with our friends again. Mum walked everywhere for a while. But it was too far so she got another car. She couldn't drive it at first, but then she started to and she could drive to the supermarket and back okay. Dad, in my dream you were the driver of the truck.'*

■ MAKE HUMOUR WORK FOR YOU

We've been working on the assumption that most of the impact of your message is in the way it is delivered. When you use humour your impact is even greater. It's commonly quoted that humour increases the audience's ability to remember by 20 per cent. Humour is powerful stuff.

- *Make it relevant*. A phrase like 'which reminds me' won't save you if there's no connection between joke and message.
- *Rehearse the joke*. Word-for-word. For once I'm only suggesting spontaneity if you're a very experienced stand-up comedian.

Now I'm going to break the eleventh commandment: 'Thou shalt not commit sacrilege by analysing the humour out of a good joke.'

Telling the essence of a good joke is usually nowhere near enough to make it funny. For example, here's a joke told in essence: A tailor drops his slice of bread and it falls jammy side up. Because he is a Jew and living in Germany he wonders how he could be so lucky, but the reason is that he put the jam on the wrong side. Side-splitting? No, of course not. In fact, you probably can't see the joke at all. That's because it depends on how you put it together.

Try this instead. Read down the left-hand column first, before you look at the analysis on the right.

... the fact is we've been lucky. Our toast has fallen jammy side up on this one.	← The link. Making the humour relevant.
Which reminds me of the little old Jewish tailor who lived in a remote village in the depths of Germany.	← *Little, old, remote village, depths*. Paint pictures with your words. Very specific, very detailed, lots of adjectives.
One day he put down his needle, made himself a slice of bread and jam and was just about to take his first bite ... when it fell on the floor — jammy side up! He was astounded.	← One day. The storyteller mode. The child in all of us feels pleasure in hearing it. ← *Jammy side up!* Emphasis. Your whole body should be involved in astonishment.
He said to himself, 'I am a Jew. In Germany. How can I have so much luck?' He went to the village elders and told them how the bread had fallen jammy side up. He said, 'I am a Jew. In Germany. How can I have so much luck?' And they were astonished.	← *Act* it. Spread your hands, raise your eyebrows. ← The same sequence will be repeated three times, building tension, and reinforcing what has to be understood for the punch-line to be funny.

They spent days puzzling over the problem	← *Act* it. Building tension.
They consulted amongst themselves, they consulted the ancient writings of the Torah, they consulted God.	← This powerful pattern of three phrases is known as the *Rule of Three*.
Then they went back to the little old tailor and said, 'We have the answer.'	
The tailor put down his needle. 'What is it?' he asked. 'I am a Jew. In Germany. How can I have so much luck?.'	← The conversation builds more tension. They didn't just arrive and deliver the answer.
And they said, 'It is because you put your jam on the wrong side of the bread!'	← Punch line right at the end, with high energy to ram it home. Never put 'they said' last.

When preparing humour, add words that build visual pictures and heighten tension, and remove words that don't.

One more point. Don't shilly-shally your way into a joke with 'Stop me if you've heard this one' or 'I hope you haven't heard this one'. Head straight into it. Yes, there's always the risk that someone who has heard it before won't be able to resist helping you out with the punch line. But don't worry — I've heard that such people go directly to a special place in hell where the coffee always arrives cold.

ABUSE THE AUDIENCE
One of the most successful forms of humour is to bend a joke so you can abuse your audience. In the West, audiences love to be abused. Why else would we have *Fawlty Towers* restaurants where customers pay exorbitantly for actor–waiters to treat them like rubbish that just blew in from the alley? It works well, as long as you follow three rules:
- The abuse must be obviously outrageous.
- The abuse must be witty.
- No reasonable person must feel belittled. Take care. Many an audience will laugh at the same time as they lower their estimation of you. These are hypersensitive days. Many are primed to be offended by any reference to any minority group.

Examples: (*To a group of surgeons*) But then what else can you expect? He's a surgeon. He suffers from love bites ... most of them self-inflicted. (*To lawyers*) It's a terrible mistake to insult a lawyer. I did it once and he was so angry he was beside himself ... you never saw such an unattractive couple. (*To a group of public speakers*) Yes, like all public speakers he's a dedicated exhibitionist. In the winter he jumps out in front of girls and describes himself.

■ TAKE ADVANTAGE OF INHERENT HUMOUR

To indulge in spontaneous, inherent humour is to take advantage of whatever happens or is said. It's not as side-splitting as a carefully crafted joke, but it's usually the most heart-warming of humour. It's a gentle humour that brings chuckles, here and there, and most clearly brings audience rapport.

You don't have to be a born comedian! I often hear people talk about wit as if you've either got it or you haven't. It's just not true. The ability to use inherent humour is easily learnt if you practise spotting and exploiting opportunities, not just in presentations but in everyday conversations. Some get a good start, growing up in families that encourage such opportunism. I didn't have that start, but I've learnt it and it's one of the skills I value most. When inherent humour knocks, let it in. It's good company. When it opens the door, go through. Or as the Americans say: roll with it.

Take advantage of the inherent humour of an event by extending it to the point of absurdity.

Ordinary events contain inherent humour you can exploit shamelessly.

- *Example:* Someone from the audience knocks over a glass and spills ice and water in his neighbour's lap. Do you say, 'Would you like me to stop a moment while you clean up?' No, you take advantage. Such as, 'If you thought he needed a shower, you could have just said!'
- *Example:* You've just told the audience, '. . . and never ever force cats to perform in front a camera. They feel the tension . . .' But why stop there? Take advantage, by extending the concept into the absurd: 'I'm telling you, if you force a cat to perform it will take your hand off at the elbow!'

Or you could play-act the unspoken cat to human conversation, looking each way at the right time. 'I don't want to.' 'Yes you do.' 'I don't want to . . .' 'You'll love it. You know you will.' 'I'm warning you.' This kind of humour doesn't demand a perfect punch line or a comedian. Let your imagination go a little more each time and it will get easier and better.

■ SIGNALS TO JOURNALISTS

If you've been in an audience with a television crew next to you videoing the speaker you might have noticed a curious pantomime. If the speaker is working without notes, or departing from speech notes, the reporter probably looks intensely focused. They'll be fixated on the speaker, eyes narrowed, listening for pearls among the words. Every now and then they'll tap the camera operator on the leg and the red light will come on, usually half-way through a sentence. Another tap, it goes off.

But if the speaker is experienced, the reporter will look very different. They'll be watching but they'll be considerably more relaxed. Now, when the speaker comes to the part they know is going to be important, watch what happens. Either they glance significantly towards the reporter, or, more likely, they'll put out a media signpost: 'And let me tell you this … [*pause, reporter taps camera operator, red light goes on*]' or 'And I can't stress this enough … [*pause*]'. I recommend the signpost method, because it's less obvious to the live audience that you are attending to needs other than their own.

■ NEVER EVER APOLOGISE FOR YOUR SPEAKING ABILITIES

'Why don't the feller who says, "I'm not a speech maker" let it go at that instead o' givin' a demonstration.' Kin Hubbard

Hubbard expressed the usually silent groan most of us utter when we hear someone apologise for their shortcomings as a speaker. A speaker such as this conveys: *I want to lower your expectations so that you judge me by an easier standard. Also, I don't want you to feel let down at the end, so I'll make you feel let down right now.* Such feelings lead to the submissive signals and words we mentioned earlier — a self-fulfilling prophecy of doom.

chapter 5

Handling audience interaction

- Dealing with questions and objections

- Handling audiences with ease and authority

'Instruments have been invented that will throw a speaker's voice more than a mile. Now we need an instrument that will throw the speaker an equal distance.'
Public Speaker's Treasure Chest.

The technique in this chapter is one of the finest ways I know of developing personal strength and authority. Also — unlike most models — exceptions are rare. It will help you handle virtually any kind of unexpected event. It will show you easy and confident handling of questions, interjections, cross-fire among the audience, aggressive comments about your message, hostility and personal attacks on you. It even works for handling attacks on you when you deserve them!

■ DEALING WITH QUESTIONS AND INTERJECTIONS

This is the basic formula for dealing with any question or interjection:
- Listen on behalf of everyone.
- Share the reply with everyone.
- Add energy.
- Accept feelings and argue facts.
- Sometimes check with the audience.

Let's look at the steps in more detail.

LISTEN ON BEHALF OF EVERYONE

Yes, rather than a technique, this first segment is a state of mind. You're there to achieve your own purposes, but unless you're tuned to the audience it might not happen. You can turn up with a message clear to you, you can deliver it as planned, but unless you're willing to adapt the words to suit the immediate needs of the audience, your message may not sink in.

What you transmit and what they receive are never identical and can be utterly different.

Have you heard the one about the boy who announced that he had taught his dog to sing? He demanded 20 cents from his brothers to see for themselves. They paid up. The boy took them to the dog and began to make hand movements like a conductor. 'Sing, Marmaduke, sing,' he commanded. The dog raised its eyelids and ears, then shut them down again and went back to sleep. The brothers complained. But the boy happily explained, 'I said I taught him. I didn't say he learned anything.'

To make sure your message is both given and received, you must welcome dynamic, two-way interaction — especially with smaller audiences.

But for many presenters, fear of questions and interjections is even greater than the fear of speaking.

In Greek mythology, Pandora carried a box, which, if opened, would release all manner of evils on the world. For many presenters, allowing something unexpected to happen is like allowing Pandora's box to be opened. The thought of an interjection is treated as a danger signal and switches on this kind of self-talk:

'Excuse me.'

Uh-oh. 'Yes?'

'I have a question.'

Oh no. A question. I hate it when people put me off my stride. I'll get flustered. It'll put me off what I prepared. What if it's something I can't handle? If I can't handle it, I'll look like a fool.

That self-talk is destructive because it turns in on itself to where fears feed and doubts double. Instead, I invite you to throw this switch in your mind.

Choose to welcome questions and interjections.

Just one catch — you have to mean it. It's very difficult to act it.

Still seem like a big ask? Think of it this way: your message has little chance of sinking in unless you can genuinely put the audience first. It's a neat irony that if you do so, you'll reap a rich harvest yourself. And now the self-talk becomes something like this:

'Excuse me.'

'You have a question?' [*Ah, good. Another opportunity for rapport. I enjoy these contributions — they help keep me in contact with the audience. And they almost always throw up things other people wanted to know anyway.*]

One more idea. Imagine yourself at a party. You're standing there talking to one person, a glass of your favourite lubricant in your hand. You're not enjoying it because the person you're talking to is boring. Which is a puzzle, because he has an interesting reputation, he's done spectacular things, and he's extremely well informed. So how can he be boring? Our perception of 'boring' or 'arrogant', or 'I don't like this bozo' often arrives when the other person is not interested in listening to or understanding us. In other words, they're no good at the first of these three points (an extension of Covey's 2-step principle):

First seek to understand.

Then seek to be understood.

Finally seek solutions or take action.

That state of mind, together with the rest of the technique, is startlingly effective. I've seen scores of trainees, once terrified of questions, discover that they had been spurning a priceless gift.

So, I hope it's clear that this section is not just about listening. You'll be listening as a representative of the whole audience with a desire to understand and respond. If you don't understand, ask questions, then repeat or paraphrase the original question to everyone if necessary (especially for large groups), then acknowledge, even if it's only with a nod.

Now let's move from state of mind to action.

SHARE THE REPLY WITH EVERYONE

This is the simplest but most crucial of the five principles. Without it, you'll find it hard to be effective. In physical terms, it's a movement of eyes, head and upper body and you'll find it easy to practise.

After the first phrase of your answer, move your eyes off the questioner and around the audience as you speak.

Now that might sound strange. Doesn't it defy normal rules of courtesy? In most European-derived cultures, weren't we taught as youngsters that it's polite to look at someone when you answer them? So we were, but for group communication that rule is inadequate. The group psychology is that when someone asks a question, it is as if the whole group adopts it and wants to know your answer even when many already know the answer.

That's so important it's worth noting this: after the first word or phrase of your answer, *it is rude to talk to the person who asked the question or gave the interjection!*

Still not convinced?

Try this thought experiment: imagine you're in the front row of an audience of 500. You ask a question, but the answer is a long one and the presenter looks at you straight down the barrel for the entire time. How do you feel? If you're not uncomfortable, I'll be amazed. The chances are you'll want to turn into a flatworm and exit under the carpet. Now, imagine that someone else asks a question. Again, the presenter answers at length only to the questioner. How do you and the other 498 feel now? Yes. Impatient. Ignored.

Now, ask yourself this. How small does the audience need to be in order to ignore this rule?

One. That's right, the psychology applies to all audiences from two to 2 000 000. It's not well known, because in small groups it's less obvious. Most presenters 'lock on' to the questioner for the entire answer and get away with it. But it's not strong, it's not authoritative and it's not right.

Let's begin with some basic examples. We'll assume you've got an audience of, say, 100, where we can't be sure everyone heard the question and the effects of the psychology are obvious. Straight-forward questions. No hidden agendas.

LARGE GROUP

A You have a question?	
Q Yes. Is the Middle East situation going to raise prices here?	← Your gaze stays on the questioner until you fully understand the question.
A *Still looking at the questioner.* You mean at the pumps?	← *Listening on behalf of everyone.* When in doubt, ask. And your stance indicates a genuine desire to understand, inclined slightly forward, questioning.

Q Yes.

A *Nod, then turn to the rest of the audience.*   ⬅ *Sharing the reply with everyone.* Looking
                                                       away from the questioner is usually the most
                                                       difficult part for beginners. But the positive
                                                       response from the audience is immediate
                                                       and so is your feeling of authoritative control.

The question is, 'Will the Middle East   ⬅ Your eyes move around the whole audience.
situation raise prices at our petrol pumps   If you succeed in 'sharing the reply with
…'   everyone', you'll find the answer not only
                                                 comes more easily, it helps you capitalise
Well, I don't know yet. In fact, I'm reluctant   and move on. Move the audience back to
to even guess until I know how the other   your track.
OPEC nations react.

Which brings me to the local political
reaction …

Now let's go to a much smaller group where it's so tempting to give the answer back to
the questioner, one-to-one. This time, you're running a meeting with half a dozen people.
We can assume everyone heard the interjection.

SMALL GROUP

A … and my feeling is that if we don't
   terminate her contract, the —

Q Excuse me Bonnie … but she's a solo
   parent, disabled, with four children under
   five. The press will make us roast of the day.

A *Nod, acknowledging contribution.*   ⬅ *Listening for everyone.* As a facilitator you
                                                   acknowledge even the interjections you disagree
                                                   with to show that you value the contribution.

   Yes, you're right.

   Turn to the others.   ⬅ *Sharing the reply.* Include the others, even
                                                   in a small group.

   But what's the alternative? She's   ⬅ The questioner never feels insulted that
   blackmailing us with her disadvantaged   you don't look at him or her again for a
   status so she can go right on doing it to the   while. Instinctively, we know that once
   same youngsters. The parents are going to   we've uttered it, it's no longer ours alone.
   get the press to roast us anyway.

   I suggest we …   ⬅ Again, the psychological momentum of
                                                   sharing the reply with everyone has
                                                   allowed you to capitalise and move on.

When a question or interjection leaves someone's lips, *the whole audience owns it.* That's true even when most of the audience disagrees with the interjection, because they will readily adopt a devil's advocate position just to find out your answer. That's why you need to make a special effort, even in a small group, to avoid being locked into the one-to-one dialogue trap.

You can return to the questioner or interjector, but only for two special reasons: first, you're giving equal attention to all of the group and they are still part of that group. Second, at the end of your answer it works well to return for a quick nod of thanks for the contribution before you move on.

ADD ENERGY

This is nothing to do with becoming high-pitched and querulous.

Show yourself to be slightly energised by the question or interjection.

Show greater interest, greater intensity, slightly greater volume, eyebrows slightly higher. Adding energy has two effects: it shows fundamental respect for the interjection or question, and it helps boost your psychological momentum even further.

Let's try that last example again, this time adding energy.

A Yes ... you're right, but what's the alternative? She's blackmailing us with her disadvantaged status so she can go right on doing it to the same youngsters. The parents are going to get the press to break out the carving knives anyway, and on us! I suggest we find her a ...	← *Sharing the reply* and *adding energy.* Greater involvement, greater intensity and interest. It adds to the psychological momentum that makes you fluent, allows you to capitalise more easily and move on.

It works. And you'll find that it gives you a state of mind that *helps the answers come to you easily.* I have seen many workshop trainees go from doubting to converted with a single success, then say things like, 'I'm much more in control, I feel more authoritative.' It's a powerful, natural method.

ACCEPT FEELINGS, ARGUE FACTS

Show that you accept all feelings — spoken and unspoken — in your manner and tone, and sometimes acknowledge them verbally.

This looks like Life Choice No. 3. In fact, you'll need all three life choices. For example you can't do this without genuinely putting audience needs first.

Treat anger, aggression, and all the other so-called negative emotions, as a gift. Hidden anger undermines you, open or partially revealed anger can be turned in your favour. This kind of thinking assumes that you have a great deal of strength deep down that you can draw to the surface. You do. It's just that the demands of ordinary everyday life often mask it until we wonder if we have it at all. It might take unusual circumstances to bring it out, but it's there, waiting for us.

A ... so we're all going to have to sign the pool cars in and out.	
Q Oh, great. *Sarcastic*	
A *Nod to interjector. Warm eyes.*	← *Listening on behalf of everyone.* Non-judgemental acceptance of a feeling. You don't feel annoyed or threatened.
I think we all hate red tape ...	← *Accepting feelings.*
Turn to audience.	← *Sharing the reply with everyone.* The sharing gives you the psychological momentum to find articulate, fluent answers.
... but, we'd all hate the alternative a lot more and we do have to stop the system being abused.	← Using the word 'hate' shows that you heard the feeling, not just the word. Your tone and demeanour show you accept feelings even when you disagree with the argument.
Now you'll find these booklets in each car ...	← Moving on.

In that example, something subtle and powerful happened.

Your tone and demeanour say YES to the person and to the feelings, while your words may say YES or NO to facts or logic.

Have you noticed strong presenters react to overt emotion like this?

A ... so that restructuring is inevitable. We're going to —	
Q Why don't you just come out with it! You're going to make some of us redundant.	← During this the presenter is listening intently, absorbing and accepting the feeling as it is revealed.
A *An emphatic forward movement of the head.* Absolutely not. There will be no redundancies. We just don't need them when ...	← *The body says yes, the words say no* and it is not a contradiction because the first accepts feelings and the second rejects facts. The two are on different planes of communication.

A forward movement of the head? A nod? It may seem more logical to shake your head at that moment. And if you want to rely just on the language of logic, it is. But a good communicator relies also on the language of feelings and speaks both simultaneously. A shake of the head in the example we've just seen could well be taken as a rejection of the fear behind the interjection.

Do you see the beauty of it? You can be assertive about disagreeing with someone, yet convey respect and cause the audience to respect you.

All right, let's raise the ante and make it a bit tougher.

SOMETIMES CHECK WITH THE AUDIENCE

Besides the obvious benefit, checking directly with the audience can often silence an aggressive interjector. It places the interjection in perspective. The interjector is confronted with the psychological weight of the audience.

A   So if you plant this variety a month earlier, you're likely to —

Q   Listen. I paid good money for that rubbish last year and I got zilch out of it.

A   *You show surprise, but nod, acknowledging the contribution. Hearing a murmur of agreement from a few of the 20 farmers present, you turn to the audience.*

← *Listening for everyone.* The nod is an acceptance of feeling, not an agreement with the facts.

Looks like others feel the same ... how many? Show me some hands? *You scan the audience.*

← *Sharing the reply with everyone.*

Three ... no, four. Anyone else? No. Okay, I don't know what that's about, but we'll need to sort it out. Perhaps the four of you would like to talk with me afterwards ... *Scan the four quickly until you get acknowledgement.*

← *Adding energy.* Accepting and reflecting the feelings. Checking with the audience. You are not showing fear or embarrassment, rather concern and interest.

All right, let's continue ...

← *Capitalising and moving on* as a facilitator. Far more important than taking aggression personally is respecting the audience's need for a constructive outcome.

Notice that when you acknowledge an aggressive interjection your manner (often just in the nod) implies, *I may disagree with your argument, but I accept your feelings.*

Now an even tougher test. Let's look at the same example again, but this time the *majority* feel aggressive and are not interested in anything but sorting out their quarrel with you.

Q Listen, I paid good money for that rubbish last year and I got nothing out of it.

A *You nod, acknowledging the contribution. But there's a strong murmur of agreement from many of the farmers. You turn to them, questioningly.*

← *Listening for everyone.* Surprised but not threatened; you're a facilitator.

← *Sharing the reply with everyone.*

A lot of you feel the same way?

There's another, stronger murmur from a clear majority, most are scowling at you, some look puzzled. One speaks.

← *Adding energy ... Accepting and reflecting the feelings. Checking with the audience.*

Q None of us are going to have that rubbish on again. You've got a nerve trying to sell it to us.

← Here's the direct aggression and personal abuse. They're questioning your integrity. But, provided your conscience is clear, you can still choose to feel secure. Why? Because you respect the audience enough to want a constructive outcome for them.

← *Listening for everyone.*

You acknowledge this contribution also with your body language (at least a nod, certainly some surprise), turning again to the audience.

← *Sharing the reply.*

A I didn't expect this. Let me check something. How many of you had problems with it? Can you indicate with your hands? *Thirteen raise hands.*

← *Adding energy. Accepting and reflecting feelings.* The concern in your tone conveys that you heard the feelings. *Checking with the audience.* By checking, you establish control and you help the audience put their feelings in perspective.

How many of you took a decent yield? *Four raise hands. A few shrug uncertainly.*

Thank you. Well, I suggest we change course. It'll be a waste of time dealing with anything else till we sort this one out. Do you agree?

← *Capitalising and moving on.* This is expert unruffled facilitation. In this case, moving on means a change in direction in response to the needs of the audience. Abandoning the prepared format like this is not a failure — it's an achievement.

A few nods, then a murmur of assent. Many look sceptical, but there's a hint of grudging respect in one or two faces.

← You may not win them, but you have certainly earned respect, even though you've not yet answered the personal accusation. Now's the time.

Before we do that, I want to tell you most strongly that I for one, and my company, had no idea of the extent of the problem.

← *Sharing the reply with everyone.* Your chances of them accepting this declaration are now excellent, because you have shown the strength of character to put their needs before your own.

Now, I'd like to see if frost susceptibility is a factor. Can you give me your experience on that? Who's out on the coastal strip?

← *Capitalising and moving on.*

Well, there's the full method. As much as suggesting technique, I've been trying to highlight the importance of your feelings and attitudes. You'll find the aggressive interjections difficult if you use the method simply as a mechanical list. But, you'll find it surprisingly easy if you open yourself to the principal feeling behind it: that you can choose to put your audience first and that by so doing you are helping yourself and rising above any sense of threat and insecurity.

Now let's apply the method to a few more situations.

HOW TO HANDLE PERSONAL HOSTILITY WHEN YOU DESERVE IT

Believe it or not, the same principles apply, provided that whatever mistake you made was done in good faith.

Let's suppose you're accused unexpectedly and you realise instantly that the accusation is right. The first thing to realise is this:

When you own up to a mistake, you do not have to choose to wear humility or indignity.

If you do choose that, you'll also be manufacturing a sour experience for the audience. Even an audience that's angry about your mistake subconsciously wants you to respond with inner strength. Yes, you will be open about the mistake, but your tone and manner are implying I choose to be bigger than any mistakes I make; my character is not affected by this experience.

Hear that word 'choose' again?

A ... so at her request I've arranged for Tania, Hans, and Peter to go to the Berlin conference.	
There's an immediate buzz. Heads turn. People look at each other in surprise and annoyance.	
A problem?	← *Listening for everyone.*
Q *Accusing tone.* I'll say. The new Head Office rules say all district managers go to Berlin.	← You are listening intently.
A How's that?	← Natural surprise.
Q We've all re-arranged our schedules. You handed us the protocol two days ago and asked us to read it carefully.	← You're puzzled as you hear this, but in no way defensive.

A *Turn to audience.* You've got a copy there?

    Several people flip through pages, one hands a page to you and points. You read. Hmm. Hand it back, turn to audience.

    Right. My apologies, everyone. I asked you to read it carefully, and I obviously didn't do so myself.

    You'll need that resolved, pronto. You might like to help yourselves to coffee while I talk to Head Office.

← *Sharing the reply* and *checking with the audience.*

← *Adding energy. Accepting and reflecting the feelings.* Open, but not an open book. Firm, authoritative tone. Perhaps even a hint of wry smile. Your character is much too strong to feel threatened by a single mistake. You are unembarrassable, even when you've made a mistake.

← *Capitalising and moving on.*

WHEN THE INTERJECTION DOESN'T WARRANT VERBAL ATTENTION

Many interjections are so fleeting, so lightweight, that it would be ludicrous to spend words on them. But the same golden rule applies.

A So, come Saturday night, Rachel and I aim to get together to —

Q Hah! *Light hearted.*

A *You continue almost without pause, raising one eyebrow, a hint of amusement in the eyes, no more than a glance at the interjector.*

    — to work out how to get everyone involved in . . .

← *Accepting.*

HANDLING THE DRUNK INTERJECTOR

I don't mean a pleasantly relaxed interjector. I mean an interjector so plastered they make the audience wince when they call out. In that state, they often won't even respond to the very obvious disapproval of the audience. Such people are on a different planet, so treat them as if they're exactly that far away. When they call out, don't show that you noticed them at all. Nothing happened. It does nothing for anyone's fundamental respect, but I've seen it sober up a drunk faster than a poke in the eye. Just don't try it on anyone other than a drunk. Or a heckler.

HANDLING THE HECKLER

The easy answer is the same as for the drunk (above). It takes a courageous and persistent heckler to continue when you and an entire crowd cause them to vanish in the psychological sense.

But, there's a better answer. Better, because it's fun. Just make sure you have a very well-nourished sense of being bigger than the occasion, that you have a good sense of humour and that you want to give as good as you get.

On all three counts, I salute John Morley, a British politician who had just finished a rousing campaign address by requesting his listeners to vote for him.

'I'd rather vote for the devil,' a heckler chimed in.

'Quite so,' Morley observed. 'But if your friend declines to run, may I count on your support?' Spontaneous and inspired. Few hecklers would have a ready answer to that one.

We can't all be like Morley, of course. But we don't need to be. You can have heckler repartee up your sleeve, ready. Here's a suggestion. A union official, John McKenzie, confronted with a gadfly heckler, told a story. And note that after the first two words to the heckler, he told the rest of the story to the whole audience. He shared the reply with everyone, coming back to the heckler at the last three words.

'You know, *[turn away from heckler to audience]* . . . I must tell you about the farm I once lived on with my mother. She was very concerned about my behaviour back then, because I didn't have much respect for the animals. In fact I even used to torment an old broken down donkey that was too stupid to run away. "One day," she said to me, "that donkey is going to come back and haunt you." *[Turn back to heckler.]* And here he is!'

It wouldn't do any harm to watch out for a few one-line heckler-killers like these:

'Does your nurse know you stopped taking the pills?'

'Now, now, you're getting a bit over-excited.'

'Yes, April the first — a very significant date for my friend here.'

And if you're wondering about fundamental respect, don't. The comments are so clearly outrageous and light-hearted, you don't compromise respect for the individual. Just be sure that it really is heckling, not a genuine question or grievance.

HANDLING THE HIDDEN AGENDA

The needles of the stinging nettle are so small they're nearly invisible, but they still bring a thoroughly unpleasant result, especially when brushed lightly. In an audience, the hidden agenda (or barely-concealed emotion) is much the same. And your first instinct is often to brush it off, though the brushing simply injects more poison into your presentation.

However, take a lesson from the goat. Tiptoe through the nettle patch and you're likely to find a goat in the middle of it, not only eating the nettle, but getting a nourishing meal from it. He's doing what anyone in the know does to handle nettle: while a light brush hurts, a firm grip hurts far less.

Grasp the nettle directly.

In the middle of a nettle patch you don't have a choice. You have to grasp the nettle and pull. Then you'll have no trouble handling what comes out.

Say you're trying to deliver a talk to government officials and social workers on the dangers of letting a child with a problem talk to anyone who believes child-abuse is rampant. But, you notice two or three expressions becoming sour. No-one makes a sound, but there are sidelong glances. Significant looks. Thin lips. The audience is disturbed by something.

Do you do anything about it?

Yes, you do. Your talk will now fail if you don't.

You pause, looking from one to another.

A Am I missing something?

← There are many ways you can ask this first question: 'There's something you want to say?', 'Some of you don't seem happy about this', 'Something you want to ask me?', 'What's happening?', and so on.

Now apply the technique. Here's an example involving heavy passions, to demonstrate how easy it is to handle as long as you are acting in good faith.

Q *A woman jumps to her feet and practically spits out her words.*

I resent your implication that innocent men get convicted as a result of social-workers' and psychologists' beliefs.

There's a buzz of support from half a dozen.

← Here's the sting of unexpectedly released emotion. But if you are *listening on behalf of everyone* with genuine and serious interest, there *is* no sting.

A *You nod, looking around questioningly.*

Looks like you're not the only one who feels that strongly.

← *Sharing the reply with everyone.*

← *Accepting and reflecting the feelings. Checking with the audience.*

A man sitting next to her speaks without rising. If anything, he's even angrier.

Q In my experience every accusation has turned out to be true! Our methods are well proven in the courts.

A So you feel that social workers are objective and not unduly influenced by their own beliefs?

← *Reflecting the feelings. Checking that you are correctly listening on behalf of everyone.*

Q That's right.

A *Nod again, looking round.* Other opinions?

← Your tone is serious, *reflecting the feelings. Checking with the audience.* You're now inviting cross-fire.

HANDLING CROSS-FIRE

Your manner and body language say you are allowing the cross-fire to happen as a useful and constructive part of your presentation. They say you're still in control and might step in any time. Notice that with this system, there is no need, ever, to feel insecure, as long as you are acting in good faith.

Audience members, direct comments to each other and to the audience as a whole.

Q1 I think he's right. My grandfather won't even stop to help a child who's fallen off her bike. He's terrified of getting accused.

← Throughout this cross-fire you have a listening look about you. You are *listening for everyone*. You're a facilitator genuinely interested in the points of view of both sides, even though one side is vehemently opposed to your message.

Q2 Rubbish. It's been proven that children simply do not lie about these things!

Q1 I agree that they usually don't lie. But their beliefs and memories are changed unwittingly by social workers who believe that child abuse is under and in every bed —

Q3 That is outrageous. We have the highest ethical standards carried out under constant senior supervision.

Q4 Your standards have all the delicacy of a bull in a china shop. Your good intentions pave the path to hell. You wreck lives.

After a few of these exchanges you hold up a hand.

All right. Thank you. Obviously some of us are in heavily entrenched positions. Even so, I want to try to ask you to consider ...'

← *Sharing the reply with everyone.* Looking after the whole audience's needs by insisting on moving on

WHEN THERE'S AN EXPERT IN THE AUDIENCE

I can see it now.

'Excuse me. I'm afraid I must take issue with your statement that Lady Margot was discourteous to Jean Harlowe ...'

Oh no, an expert! She's going to be an expert! She'll know more than me!

'In fact, when Jean Harlowe said, "It's a pleasure to meet you Lady Margot", she pronounced it with a 't' and Lady Margot's reply was "No my dear, it's Margot. The 't' is silent as in Harlowe."'

The audience laughs.

'Uh ...' *What a disaster! She's probably knows the hour and the day that Harlowe and Margot sneezed! They'll all think this woman should be up here instead of me. They'll think I'm a pretender! They'll think I'm a charlatan!* 'Uh ... good point ... Well, returning to the subject at hand ...'

That kind of self-talk shows how disasters are made by the way we choose to respond, not by what is thrown at us. And true, roll-the-eyeballs presentation disasters loom when we choose to feel threatened. We make such choices when we turn in on ourselves as opposed to putting the audience first. Instead, quite deliberately, choose not to be threatened. Instead, choose to focus on what the audience needs. How? First, let's get the self-talk right.

'Excuse me. I'm afraid I must take issue with your statement that Lady Margot was discourteous to Jean Harlowe.'

'Of course. Go ahead.' *Maybe she can add a useful perspective.*

'In fact, when Jean Harlowe said, "It's a pleasure to meet you Lady Margot", she pronounced it with a 't' and Lady Margot's reply was "No my dear, it's Margot. The 't' is silent as in Harlowe."'

The audience laughs and you laugh with them. *Great! What a gift.* 'Thank you, I stand corrected. You seem well-informed on those two.'

'Well, yes, I've read a bit.' *Yes. An expert. The audience are going to find this funny, coming along to a talk on Lady Margot and finding someone who knows more than the presenter.*

'Well, if I can't answer a question, I'm going to ask you.' For a large audience, you can easily capitalise now and move on. *(With warmth)* 'All right ... Let's go on to Lady Margot's last years ...'

Look back at that self-talk. The most important word was perspective. The audience did not come to hear facts about Lady Margot. They came to hear your perspective on Lady Margot. The difference means that it doesn't matter a jot if the interjector is a walking Encyclopaedia Britannica.

Suppose the interjector accepts an invitation to take part in the presentation. You are still running things. You're facilitating an interesting show for the audience in which your perspective contains the perspective of the interjector. And let's take it to an extreme to make the whole point. Suppose you discover that sitting right there in your audience is someone whose perspective would be so valued by the audience they would be very disappointed not to take full advantage of it. The answer is easy if you are open and audience-centred.

'Ladies and gentlemen, I don't think any of us realised Henry Zeigfeld was going to be here tonight. I think you'll agree that it would be very disappointing not to take advantage of him and get his perspective. Mr Zeigfeld, how would you feel about taking a few minutes to talk to us about the ... ?'

Still in control. Still facilitating. Still putting the audience first. And even though you know zip compared to the bottomless well of knowledge called Henry Zeigfeld, the audience will come away admiring your leadership skills.

So, was there ever any need to feel threatened? No.

Here's one special wrinkle. What do you do when you know there's an expert in your audience even before you begin? And you know they know more than you.

Acknowledge their presence.

You might squeeze it in at the end of the introduction: 'I want to show you that by speeding up the day-night cycle for battery hens, theoretically, you could reach a lay rate of 24 eggs a day. But before I begin, I would like to give a special welcome to Martha Lutyens. Most of you will know that Martha has a great deal of expertise in the biological effects on humans when working in an accelerated day–night chicken cycle environment. Martha, perhaps you could add your perspective from time to time as we go?'

Battery hens aside, the three most important points are:

- take pleasure in acknowledging expertise
- be willing to take advantage of the expertise
- fold the expert into the context of your perspective.

WHEN YOU DON'T KNOW THE ANSWER

When you don't know, say — *cheerfully* — 'I don't know'.

It really is as simple as that, though it might need a follow up. You could check with the audience. Say, 'I don't know, can anyone answer that one?' But if no-one knows, undertake to find out. And did you pick up the most important word there? *Cheerfully*. The point is that the audience is much more wired to your personal strength than to whether or not you know something. The fact that you don't know is almost inconsequential. Say the same words in embarrassment and they will turn from you.

'Excuse me. When was that study completed?'

'I don't know. Can anyone answer that one?' *Silence*. 'No,' *cheerfully*, 'can't help you.'

When the farewelled one bites back

You're farewelling a staff member and they take the opportunity to criticise the company. It's commonplace during economic upheaval, when many don't know at the beginning of the day whether they'll have a job when they go home. From middle management down, many are working harder and longer for more ulcers and less pay. Some take the opportunity to let rip at the company letting them go. A tense moment, but the solution is not difficult.

In the following example, accepting feelings is by far the most important component. And remember that accepting feelings does not imply acceptance of the facts being offered.

The process reduces tension. His intention was to express feeling and you acknowledged precisely that without getting sucked into debating the face value of the words.

Of course a really angry person may persist for longer. If so, become assertive about the about time and place, but let your manner still carry understanding and fundamental respect.

A Blaine, on behalf of us all, I want to wish you the very best with whatever you tackle next.	
Q Is that so? Well that's a right load of hypocrisy. If this company wished me well they wouldn't have made me redundant, would they? I work here for 30 years and those heartless bastards in head office still think I'm a statistic. I'm the fifth one this year. How bloody short-sighted to waste all this experience and get someone younger so they can pay them less.	← During this tirade, *listening on behalf of everyone*. Acknowledge occasionally with small nod. This is no time to feel got at.
A Blaine … *Turn to audience with occasional glances to Blaine.* I don't think there's anyone here who doesn't know that you're going through a rough time. None of us would find it easy … You said you'll probably have a go at market gardening and all of us here really do wish you the very best of success with that, or whatever else you turn your hand to. Now, let's go through to the cafe, the afternoon tea will be ready and waiting.	← *Sharing the reply with everyone.* ← *Adding energy. Accepting feelings. Checking with the audience* by raising eyebrows in questioning manner. You could attempt to answer the accusation, but it's probably not necessary. Non-judgmental recognition and acknowledgment of feeling is the most important factor.

HANDLING QUESTION TIME

To initiate questions, ask an open question. For example, 'What questions do you have?' If you ask a closed one like, 'Do you have any questions?', there might be an awkward silence, which helps your charisma as much as a dollop of cold porridge. Don't say, 'I've got time for two more questions,' because that will inhibit your audience. Instead, tell them cheerfully, 'I've got 90 seconds. I'll answer all your questions in that time.'

Audiences usually dislike judgements about questions. But it depends on your motive. If you say the usual, 'I'm glad you asked that question' or 'That's a good question,' in a flat tone, it telegraphs to the audience that you're thinking *God, how can I answer that! I wish you would shut up and stop bothering me*. The audience reads such thoughts in a nanosecond. But don't get the wrong idea. If you are genuinely very enthusiastic about the question, you can say 'That's a good question', and sound as though you mean it.

But in general, it's this:

> **Don't make value judgements (positive or negative) about questions or interjections.**

ACT ON THE NEEDS OF THE AUDIENCE

Everything I've said so far implies it, but it's worth saying directly. Too many speakers ignore obvious audience needs just so that they can get through the presentation. The moment you start speaking, you're running the whole show. You're a facilitator of everything happening now.

- Is the audience too hot? Too cold? Ask them and act.
- Are they hungry, thirsty, jaded by too many speeches? Acknowledge it.
- Do some seem to be having difficulty hearing, seeing? Act on it.
- Perhaps they appear to be puzzled about something. Ask them.
- Is there something they haven't understood? Ask them.
- Is there some kind of restlessness you don't understand? Understand by asking.

chapter 6

Handling formal or special occasions

- Formal presentations

- Informal presentations

'When a man retires and time is no longer a matter of urgent importance,
his colleagues generally present him with a watch.'
R.C. Sheriff

■ HANDLING FORMAL PRESENTATIONS

Some special occasions are either too short for the standard preparation method or they have their own particular demands on structure. So this section is essentially mechanical, often with fail-safe steps that may help with preparation. They should make no difference at all to the performance skills we've talked about. I'll make these steps as full as possible, though you'll often come across situations where you can skip steps out.

FORMAL SALUTATIONS

If you were to have a bad dream about it, it might go like this: you open your mouth to speak, but you only get as far as, 'Your Holiness ...' when you notice that the entire audience is composed of people wearing braid, ribbon and heavy golden metal. They all have telephones in front of them, and they all have fingers poised, ready to dial lawyers should you damage their sense of importance. In fact, salutations never need be a problem. Solve it in advance:

- Ask the organiser whether the occasion really warrants formality. His Worship the Mayor, Sir Terence Higginbottom won't thank you for singling him out for formal salutation as you launch into the nineteenth hole pep talk.
- Ask the organiser for the correct salutations and order. If in doubt, list the VIPs in order of rank, highest first.
- Check the spelling and pronunciation of unfamiliar names.
- Don't allow formality to dehumanise those acknowledgments. Remember that those people, under all their titles, letters and braid, are also real people. They need to see the same warmth in your eyes that you would have for anyone you met in the corridor. Say Your Holiness, Your Majesty, Your Worship the way you would say Mrs Smith, Miss Harper, Mr Peabody.

For the rest of this chapter, watch for the common elements. Once you grasp them, you'll get a feeling for the whole business. From then on you'll never need a guide.

INTRODUCING A SPEAKER

The audience needs you to put perspective on what they're about to hear and who they're about to hear it from.

- Introduce the topic, explaining its importance to the audience.
- Introduce the speaker, explaining that person's connection to the topic. Give the speaker's qualifications or experience, but also give a personal introduction. You may need to ask around to find a personal, illustrative anecdote.

As you all know, the recent rudder control failure and the near tragedy has put the

←*Introducing topic*. Explaining importance to audience.

whole of our industry under a cloud. It only takes one incident like this to endanger the reputation we've built up. And I think you'd agree with me that the best protection the public have and we have is to increase our efforts to learn more and make sure it never happens again.

I'd like to introduce you to Sybil Schreiber from Seattle. You all know of her impressive experience and international reputation in hydraulic control systems. But you may not know that Sybil was once a stunt flier. Her party trick was to stand on the wing of a Pitt Special, controlling ailerons and rudder with extension wires. But you'll be glad to hear that her safety skills have developed beyond number eight fencing wire. Could you please welcome Sybil Schreiber.

← *Introducing the speaker.* Explaining connection. Speaker's qualifications. Personal insight.

Don't upstage, gazump or oversell

It's always a mistake to try to impress the audience with your own performance abilities when introducing a speaker. That's upstaging and it's seen as extremely discourteous. If in doubt, tone your performance down while keeping your natural warmth.

Gazumping is giving the speech the speaker is about to give! It can be very tempting if you get into your enthusiastic stride. It has led to some caustic comments by speakers about how little there is left to say.

Also, in your enthusiasm, don't oversell the speaker. 'And I'd like you to welcome Jimmy Jones who is the most thrilling speaker in Australia today and I'm sure he's going to give us the most exciting talk of our lives.' Say that and Jimmy Jones will go home afterwards to stick pins in a wax dummy that looks like you.

THANKING A SPEAKER

The audience needs you to put an audience-centred perspective on what they've just heard and (sometimes) on the person they've heard it from. Notice that with the method below, there is never any need to praise a speaker for giving a good speech when it wasn't.

- During the speaker's talk, listen for something that moves the audience's feelings; interest or insight, surprise, delight, interest, shock, horror, and so on. No matter how bad the speech itself, there is always something.
- When you speak, re-visit the specific part you picked out. Say how it affected the audience. You may want to own those feelings personally, but you'll also need to imply audience involvement.

- Move from specific to general, reflecting the new perspective given to the audience.
- Thank the speaker.

Rolf, I must say that I was surprised and delighted that it's now possible to save trees that have been almost completely ringbarked. I'm sure no-one here missed the significance for native saplings in deer country, and I think some of us will be asking you for more details over coffee shortly. In fact, you have given us a great deal of insight into the art and science of native bush management generally. A most valuable talk, and I'm sure everyone here will join me in expressing our thanks.	← Revisiting something that involved audience feelings. ← Moving from specific to general. ← Thanking the speaker.

The process still works if the audience disagreed with the whole speech. You can always find something that added perspective, and therefore value. When the audience and you feel nothing but extreme opposition to everything said, you can still truthfully say, 'Dougal, as you've obviously noticed, many of us don't accept your argument. But I think those of us who argued the most would be the first to appreciate the fact that you have helped us understand your point of view. So on behalf ...'

Again, be careful of upstaging. And this time don't over-thank. Effusive praise for what the speaker knows was barely passable will be embarrassing for everyone.

FAREWELLING A STAFF MEMBER OR COLLEAGUE

Here's a classic mistake.

Chief executive, Peter Pallins, farewells employee, Simon Smith, who is thoroughly disliked. Peter is also personally glad to see Simon go. So he makes it a grudging farewell, in the sense of omission. The smiles are there, but as a blatant mask. The good wishes are there, but breathtakingly short. Everyone knows that Simon is being damned with a faint-hearted presentation. But to Peter Pallins amazement, he discovers a bad feeling being projected back at him from his own staff. He doesn't get the warm vibes he thought he would be getting from everyone else who was glad to see Simon Smith depart.

Saints are not over-represented in the population. Few people earn unreserved accolades when they leave the company. So when the audience watches you farewell one of their colleagues, part of each person is thinking, *I wonder how I'll get farewelled when I leave?*

On top of that, the audience is aware of another dimension to the farewell. They are part of an organisation that is saying good-bye to part of itself. So, suddenly, a new feeling emerges. Much though they dislike Simon, *as an audience they want him farewelled with fundamental respect*. Managers who ignore that do so at their peril. At a farewell, your leadership qualities are being weighed and balanced in a way you won't find on any other occasion.

With fundamental respect you can gracefully farewell anyone without lying. You can refer to disagreements, even blazing rows, with no loss of respect, though of course such references mustn't be lengthy.

As you speak in front of the person your 'self-talk' should be like this: *I want to give you the best and most dignified farewell possible. By doing so, I don't just honour you, I honour everyone in this room including myself.*

- Research — find an incident or story about the person leaving that shows a positive insight on their character. There's always something. You might have to research their private life through friends to find something suitable, though friends are usually more than willing.
- Use that incident to give a personal, constructive insight on the person leaving.
- If there are major negative feelings associated with the person, and if the audience is aware of them, refer to them in a non-judgmental way. 'As you know, Henry and I haven't seen eye to eye on every issue ... even so, I have valued the way Henry ...' Such openness is important, so that no-one goes away referring to you as a hogwash pusher.
- Outline the history of that person in your organisation, highlighting their achievements. If appropriate, talk about the constructive influence that person has had on your organisation. Tell illustrative anecdotes.
- Tell the audience their future plans.
- Make the presentation, and wish them well for the future.

When you know the person well, it can be tempting to run a joke or two at their expense. But beware, a joke that would have them and everyone else rolling in the aisles around a canteen table won't always work at a farewell. If you're in doubt, ask yourself 'Does the joke diminish that person's stature with this audience?' If the answer is 'yes', leave it out. Dignity is everything at a farewell. Use wit, but if it's a 'put down' you'll diminish your own stature, even in the eyes of the very people who laugh out loud at your joke.

When the farewelled one bites back
See page 97.

When it's you being farewelled
When you are being farewelled, the form to observe is clear.
- Thank the person expressing the farewell.
  Then, either:
- Express gratitude to the company and any relevant individuals. Say what being with the company has meant to you. (That could be described as the 'correct form'.)

or:

- Speak your mind about the company, expressing feelings in a controlled manner. Be seen to be bigger than your own feelings and in command of them. Even if your feelings are negative, still convey warmth to individuals present. If that's too hard, don't leave out fundamental respect, which should survive all differences.
- Say what you're going to do with the gift.
- Say what your plans are. Or, if they've been mentioned already, add some personal insight to them. Make people smile. It's their last feeling about you before you leave.

PRESENTING AND RECEIVING AWARDS

When you're presenting an award tell your audience something real about the recipient.

The presentation speech

Demonstrate warmth and interest in the recipient:

- Tell a story or anecdote that makes a point about the recipient's qualities.
- Relate those qualities to the award or presentation. The origin of the award may be relevant. Very often the person who established it did want to recognise particular qualities in a recipient.
- Outline what the recipient did to earn the award.
- Present the award.

When you're on the receiving end, be genuine, but not matter-of-fact.

The acceptance speech

'Ladies and gentlemen, I feel humbled and overwhelmed to be here . . .'

Oh dear, oh dear! How many times have we heard that? Be careful. If it's not obviously heartfelt, it comes across as a cliché of stunningly boring proportions. But the most effective acceptance speech I have ever seen was that of the young New Zealander, Anna Paquin, receiving her Oscar in 1994. When she opened her mouth to speak, nothing came out but strangled gasps. Now she was overwhelmed, and so obviously genuine that she endeared herself to millions.

If you're not so affected, try this:

- Thank the person who presented it to you. If appropriate, thank the organisers.
- Give the audience an insight into what motivated you.
- Tell them what you'll do with the award. Paint a picture, perhaps say where you're going to place it: on the mantel-piece, etc.
- Tell them what's next for you. For example, if you've won a road race, you might tell them that you don't intend to touch your running shoes again for three weeks. It'll take that long to get them through the decontamination unit.

OPENING FUNCTIONS

These are the steps to follow when you are opening a function:

1. Thank whoever introduced you.

2. Give your reasons for wanting to be here. If you don't want to be here, this is not the time to discharge honesty like a blunderbuss. Find something specific about the function that you find interesting and say so. Nor is it enough to vaguely suggest that everything will be interesting. The audience is looking for your personal and specific expression of interest.

3. Tell the audience the significance of the function. Tell them who will benefit from it.

4. Thank the organisers.

5. Officially declare the function open.

■ FUNERALS

In British-derived cultures, there have been countless funerals where the departing spirit must have looked around in amazement at the rigidly 'brave' faces and listened with incredulity to the glowing tributes and said, 'I think I'm at the wrong funeral'.

On the earthly side of the veil, the combination of 'stiff upper lip' and false tribute has wrought untold, lasting psychological damage on loved ones who never got to grips with one of the main reasons for a funeral. It's a chance to grieve openly with community support. The single most distressing thing heard at funerals is the approving comment, 'Aren't they bearing up well?'

Fortunately for collective sanity, that's changing. A funeral is the place for tears and weeping and other expression of feelings.

My partner, Sue, remembers what must be one of the best-conducted funerals in recent years. An eight-year-old boy had died by accident. He was a well-known lad with a normal eight-year-old's mixture of charm and mischief. The funeral service was held at his school. His desk was brought outside for the service, complete with books and chair. The children filed past his open coffin, many of them weeping. His brother said, 'He was a pest sometimes but I loved him anyway'. His sister shouted at him directly, 'Daniel, I'm really angry with you for going! I just wanted you to know that'. His father cried, his mother read from Kahlil Gibran. 'Your children are not your children. They are the sons and daughters of Life's longing for itself.' Then, every child in Daniel's class released lighter-than-air balloons so that he could have company getting to heaven.

Try some of the following points:

• *Sometimes speak directly to the departed.* Even if you're one who doesn't believe in life after death, consider this. You'll be speaking to the part of the deceased that lives vividly in the minds of the audience in front of you. You'll be honouring them and the deceased's memory.

- *Tell stories.* Find anecdotes that illustrate a point. Use gentle humour, sometimes directly to the one who's died. 'Pierre, do you remember that time you got us thrown out of the Sistine Chapel? You'd smuggled in a loaf of bread but the crumbs kept dropping out. Well, I hope you've been more successful this time.'
- *Express your feelings directly.* Not, 'Janine was good with children.' when it could be 'I love the way Janine dealt with children.' Better still, 'Janine, I really loved the way you dealt with children.' Feelings, crudely expressed but offered directly in good faith, are worth more than the most expensive casket. Imagine this, said in tears, 'I wish you were still here to clean me out at poker, you old bastard!'

  If you were close to the one who died, allow yourself to shed tears, even while speaking. Tears honour the one who is going and everyone present.
- *Express positive and negative feelings.* 'Stephen, I hated you for years over how you treated Ruth. I didn't want to go on feeling like that. But the trouble is, I never got a chance to tell you until now. Well, I could have made a chance, but it was hard to do. Now I want to say that ...'

  There's more dignity for the departed in honesty than there is in a whitewash. If you're going to pretend that you always liked the person or that they suddenly assumed a halo when he or she died, you might as well change their name when you refer to them. It's false and does nothing for their memory. Besides, if you have an emotional debt to the person then a whitewash covers over your own dry rot which will continue to eat away at you.
- *Sometimes refer to the human frailties of the deceased.* Not that you should trot out a whole list; whatever that person has done it would give the frailties too much importance. But you can refer to them briefly, sparingly.

■ SPEECHES FOR FAMILY AND FRIENDS

Weddings, twenty-firsts, anniversaries, birthdays, re-unions, success celebrations and many others can easily be dealt with using the standard preparation method. There are some refinements however, that you may find useful.

FORMALITY AND INFORMALITY

If you live in an egalitarian society, this can be a difficult one. In fact it's ironic; many people believe that a family 'do' is one occasion when you can throw formality out the window, but the same people often find themselves better satisfied by a little formal 'pizzazz'. As we saw earlier, formality lends importance. If you reject it out of hand, you might be depriving the family stars of some of the special feeling that should go with the function. A formality like 'I call on you to charge your glasses to toast the young couple' may mean a very special moment for that couple, even though the same couple express little respect for the 'establishment'. And that's often a lesson for the younger generation: however much you might dislike formality, it might go down very well indeed with older people.

But, whatever you decide, never mistake the formal trappings for the heart of the message.

Formalities are the fanfare, not the message.

In other words, once you've uttered the formal words, go back to talking informally, to real people, to make your message.

Ladies and gentlemen, it's my pleasant duty to propose the toast to Mum and Dad as they leave for Patagonia.	← Formal flourish to lend importance to individuals on their special occasion.
Pause	← The pause flags the shift to informality.
Mum, I can't resist this, I'm going to tell everyone what you said fifteen years ago when ...	← Simple, informal, direct. Talking to real people
Oh no ... you remembered!	
I certainly did. When I was heading off to the Andes, you know what Mum said to me? She said, 'Are you out of your mind?' (laughter) So on behalf of everyone here I want to wish a couple of fine people a wonderful trip even though they are obviously already out to lunch. Mum and Dad.	

TELL STORIES, ANECDOTES

They work well in any speech, but for family and friends, stories and anecdotes are an even more powerful resource. Mentally collect stories about your family and friends.

Here's a suggestion if you have young children. Get a sturdy notebook and record the funny things they do and say, recording the date they happened. In my family, that notebook has become a prized source of laughter as our boys read glimpses of their past. They're so proud of the notebook, they show their friends. When Sam gets married, I'm going to publicly warn the bride about the day he destroyed a dishwasher, a window and a briefcase, and broke a hammer on the piano. When discovered, *he* ticked *us* off. He wagged his finger at us and said, 'You don't shout at me, you don't send me to sit on the stairs, I go sit on the stairs myself.' Yes, the boys make protesting noises about our plan, but Sue and I know very well that they love the idea.

Don't just tell a story and leave it at that. It must be related to what follows. Tell the story, give it a point.

I'll always remember the time Annette waded into a crowd of young hoods who were tormenting a chap with Downs Syndrome. Stood right in the middle of them with her arm round the victim, cutting them to ribbons with her tongue. Half their size, she was. They just stood there with their mouths open.	← Telling the story.
That was courage. I was so proud of her. And I'm proud of Annette now and not a bit surprised to see her taking on a challenge like this ...	← Giving it a point.
OR	
Tomàs, I hope you weren't expecting a peaceful life with my daughter ...	← Making the point in advance.
Well forget it. I'm warning you now, when you have a shower, *lock the door*! When she was this high, she burst in on me washing my hair in the shower and asked at the top of her voice, 'What means God?' I put my head out of the water with the brilliant reply, 'What?'	← Telling the story.
And she said, 'If God doesn't get food does he die?' So I said, 'Can this wait?' So then she looks at the natural run-off situation and announces loudly that Daddy is doing pees in the shower! And you wouldn't believe who was in the house right then, listening to all that.	

BUT IS IT FUNNY?

Family gatherings can be excruciatingly painful if the speaker gets the jokes wrong. Time and again I've seen good atmospheres soured, with smiles becoming more and more frozen as the so-called funny stories go on. Some speakers hear laughter — even embarrassed laughter — and take it as approval to continue along the same horrible path.

The test is the same as for farewells. If the story is going to make them look human, fine. If it's going to make them look small, leave it out. You'll need to be influenced by your knowledge of the person as much as the story itself.

EXPRESSIONS OF AFFECTION

It's easy to be so carried away by the process of giving an entertaining and interesting message that you forget the most important message of all. Ideally, family occasions are an expression of love more than a matter of duty. In some way, your message has to convey that. Many people find expressions of affection or love difficult, even in private and with immediate family. Families are the poorer for it. The same goes for many social gatherings, where an expression of affection has potential for enriching everyone present.

If you live in a family that's uneasy with open displays of feeling, here's a way you can do so with reasonable ease at a family and friends gathering: deliberately give it a touch of formality. I've seen it done well by a friend at his father's eightieth birthday. He tapped his glass with a spoon. 'Excuse me everyone. I would just like to say a word. Dad, we're not a demonstrative family, I know. We don't usually tell each other our feelings about anything. But I think this is one time when it's right for us to tell you that we love you . . . and that we hope your ninetieth birthday will be even better than this one.'

chapter 7

Presenter's toolkit

- Activities

- Checklists

- Quotable quotes

activity **1** *visualisation*

Our beliefs about ourselves are extremely powerful. Beliefs create reality. Change those beliefs and — it's not hard — you change the reality. A word of caution though. Don't treat this exercise like an affirmation that you mumble or flick through endlessly in the hope of change. Patterns of words and pictures in the brain will only reprogram your subconscious if they contain the essential catalyst: your feelings.

How to approach
Take the phone off the hook, sedate the children and find a quiet spot. Play music that inspires you. The important parts of what follows are:
- detail: get as much detail in as you can — colours, textures, movements, sounds
- frequency: do the exercise often
- feelings: the essential catalyst. Deliberately encourage the feelings involved. The emotions you create here are the strongest force for turning the imagined into reality.

What to visualise
Picture yourself standing in front of a likely audience. Picture the setting. Picture the walls, with hangings, the curtains, the floor. What's the texture of the carpet? What's the design? Picture the audience, with all the texture and weave and colour of their clothes. Now put expressions on their faces. They're looking at you and listening to your words with considerable interest. You begin to feel a quiet buzz of satisfaction. You know you're performing well.

You recognise some faces of people you know. Give them names. You're performing so effectively, with such confidence and authority that many have small grins of enjoyment. Others are giving those almost imperceptible nods that indicate understanding and appreciation. What you're saying is sinking in!

Think ahead. Hear in your mind the words of relatives, friends, colleagues, bosses when they say to you, 'Well done', 'Good job', 'Enjoyed that!' Your buzz of satisfaction becomes an inner thrill of enjoyment. You feel strong. You have power to influence people.

Finally, finish with a flourish and leave with applause ringing in your ears. You have entertained them, persuaded them, convinced them, inspired them. You have the power to influence people.

Time to do some more subconscious programming. 'Let go of the bush!' is one of the powerful keys to personal flow you can try on for yourself. It stands for letting go of all your fears and self-doubt and letting yourself fly.

Try this imagination exercise.

When

At quiet times of the day, as often as you can, work through this exercise with as much conviction as you can muster. The way you feel when you do the exercise is central to its success.

What

In your mind, place yourself in front of an audience. As you speak, deliberately think up all the doubts you have. Get as much detail as you can. Deliberately let your doubts conjure up awkward body language, dropping your notes, losing your place, stuttering. Watch your fears generate everything that goes wrong. While still trying to speak, watch the effect on the audience.

Now

Laugh. Tell yourself something like, This rubbish is just getting in the way. Why am I hanging on to it? I'll let it go. All at once. Imagine it forming into the shape of a bush over your head, then open up your hands and let it go.

Relax and enjoy yourself! So obvious, so effective. Ask yourself this: Does the audience see me enjoying myself? Or do they see me joyless, flat or tense? Is my face set in stone? If you get the wrong answer, tell yourself, 'I can only win now if I start to enjoy it.' If you're enjoying yourself, so will the audience.

Another powerful performance key is the call to change our focus from an inward one to an outward, audience-centred focus.

See if you can persuade three or four friends to pretend to be an audience for five minutes. Get their feedback once you've tried the exercise.

What to do

Speak only when you are looking directly at your audience. Make sure the whole audience gets the benefit of your attention, but avoid 'carriage return' jerkiness with your eyes. Adopt a manner that says, 'I'm interested in how you're taking this in'.

Listen to the audience as you speak. Listen with your whole being: ears, eyes, mind. Your interaction with the audience is two-way even when their lips are still! They're speaking loudly with their own body language, thoughts and feelings. Alter your body language to be attentive to the audience. Not hand cupped to ear, but something much more subtle. Incline your upper body and head slightly forward. *Become interested, look interested, be interested* in how your message is going down.

How was the feedback? Were you able to vividly imagine getting out of your own head? How was your gut reaction? How did your reactions compare with those for key one? Does the concept of getting out of your head do anything for you?

activity 4 | doing the corridor test

This is a useful tool for learning how to avoid the Language of Importance.

Scan through one of your medium-length prepared presentations and jot down in the left-hand column all the phrases or words for which you suspect there is a perfectly good 'corridor' version. Then ask yourself: 'How could I have said this if I met just one of my audience in the corridor?' and put the solution in the right-hand column.

Next time you prepare a presentation, try to reach for the simpler options first.

LANGUAGE OF IMPORTANCE	LANGUAGE OF REAL COMMUNICATION

activity 5 — talking to real people

The way you say something to an assembled group of people — however large — shouldn't be too different from the way you'd say it to an individual one-to-one. Don't think 'I'm speaking to an audience', think 'I'm speaking to people, real people'.

Explain the idea to a friend and ask them to be your audience. Deliver a few sentences.

Ask
- How stuffy was the language?
- How natural did I sound?
- Did I sound personal or remote?
- Did I speak to real people?
- Did I pass the corridor test?

Try this

With your next real audience, use the word 'you' as if you were talking to a single person.

Strongly imagine yourself in the middle of your speech or presentation, asking yourself the corridor test question. Say 'thank you', rather than 'I would like to express my gratitude'; and 'if you were to . . .' rather than 'if one were to . . .'

How was that? What are your gut-level reactions to the key 'Talk to real people'? How did they compare with those of the previous keys?

activity 6 | *projecting real warmth*

Here's a simple experiment you can conduct for yourself.

What to do

Watch a bulletin of television news. As you watch each spokesperson interviewed, ask yourself:

- who has the most natural warmth in their eyes?
- who do you like the most?
- who do you listen to most easily?
- Who are you most likely to remember tomorrow?

Very often it'll be the same person for all four.

Why?

Speakers who are able to project genuine warmth and smile from the eyes when appropriate, win audiences' trust and affection. This is because their warmth tells their audience they like being where they are, doing what they're doing — they are demonstrating their liking for their audience.

Do you like the people in your audience? Allow that liking to show. Do you like your message? Do you believe in it? Is it worth convincing your audience? If the answer is yes, allow that thought to generate your natural warmth. Is it bad news? Maybe you don't even believe in the message, but you have to deliver it anyway. If so, show appropriate gravity but don't abandon your natural warmth. You could make it show by thinking of your audience. Can you show warmth for them?

activity 7 · passing the passion test

Try this

- *Be keen to explain*. Practise part of your presentation on an honest friend or colleague. Show that you're keen to get the message across by putting more energy into your eyes, your expression and your body language. What you have to say matters and you're going to get that across. Now ask your friend if your keenness to explain was underdone or overdone.

- *Act enthusiasm in front of the friend*. Act yourself delivering part of your speech with such enthusiasm that you think it's just 'over the top'. Ask your friend if it was. If so, by how much? Could you put in even more enthusiasm?

- *Read a story to a child* and indulge your repressed desire to be the next Lawrence Olivier. Deliberately act the part of a storyteller with all the emphasis, eyebrow-raising and 'ups' and 'downs' in tone of voice. Then go back to rehearsing something serious, retaining as much of the story-telling range as possible. Again, try it out on someone, with feedback. Most of us are poor judges of how far we can increase our own tonal range before being laughed at. Your child will love it and adult audiences are hardly any different.

- *Practise smiling with your eyes only*. Practise allowing warmth to show without smiling with your mouth. Imagine you're in front of your best friend. What does that do to your expression? Nothing? Try your very best friend. You'll find it affects particular muscles round your eyes and temples. Let it. Lean slightly forward. You mean business and you're going to take pleasure in it.

Look back at what you've tried. Which idea gave you the strongest gut-level response? How does it compare with your response to the other keys?

activity 8 — getting on the front foot

This is a popular key for taking control of the message, the audience and the situation. Here, the body language agrees with the metaphor of being on the front foot or having the advantage, making it all the more powerful.

What to do

Use a mirror, or talk a trustworthy friend into simulating an audience for you. Start speaking deliberately on the back foot — that is deliberate stumbles, deliberate hesitations, deliberate faltering of eye contact.

Now follow these steps:

1. Recognise you are on the back foot.
2. Recognise that you can choose to change the situation.
3. Command yourself with the key. Say to yourself: *Enough of that! Now I'll move onto the front foot, taking control of myself and the situation.*
4. Move physically, then mentally. Change your body language first, then take your determination with it.

Try this

If you're standing, shift your weight forward slightly; if you're seated, incline further forward with your upper back straight, perhaps your forearms on the table. Follow through by looking the audience in the eye, increasing your energy level and showing your keenness to get the message across. Let your upper body, arms and facial muscles move freely.

This activity might well feel artificial, but you'll be laying real advance tracks in your mind for the next real audience.

How did it go? How does your gut-level response compare with other performance keys?

activity 9 relaxation exercises

Try these exercises to relax you before a presentation.

Connection breathing

Empty your lungs. Breathe in slowly and deeply through your nose, not expanding your chest, but pushing out your belly button instead. Hold for two seconds. Hold for two more seconds. Now exhale very slowly, this time through your mouth. When half the air is gone, partially block the flow of air by pressing your lips close together (like a flute player) so that you have to tense your stomach muscles to keep exhaling. Now keep exhaling until you don't have even a whisper of air left.

Repeat the exercise three times, and use your imagination. On the inhale, visualise lines of energy flowing from the audience to you. On the exhale, push the lines of energy out through your feet, through the ground and up into the audience.

Doctors will tell you that this type of breathing acts on the vagus nerve, which acts on the heart, slowing it. Clearly, it also affects the oxygenation of the blood. And if you're willing to flex your beliefs, you may be able to accept that the exercise gently reminds mind and biochemical system of the subtle connections between you, your inner resources and your audience.

Throat relaxation

Relax your throat. Does your throat feel tight and your voice sound as if it has been squeezed out through a strainer?

Find a quiet spot and hum at a pitch that makes the soft area under your chin vibrate. As you do so, allow the vibrations to spread a feeling of relaxation through your throat and down towards your shoulders.

or

Tilt your head back and push your jaw at the ceiling for a few seconds. You should feel tension in the muscles under your chin. Also, put a couple of fingers over your bottom teeth and pull slowly but firmly downward, putting pressure on the hinge of the jaw.

Smoothly increase and decrease the pressure.

activity 10 — the power of the pause

If you're not convinced that pauses are necessary, try this mind experiment.

What to do

1. Imagine sitting in the audience watching yourself as the presenter. Every now and then you see that replica of yourself drop their eyes away from yours and start talking to their notes as if the paper were listening! And they keep on talking. They don't allow even the slightest pause to let you take in what they just said!

2. Now imagine that the replica of yourself does something different. When they need to look at the paper, they stop talking before they break eye contact and, with complete confidence, they get their information, raise their eyes again and don't speak until they have firm eye contact with you.

Your call

Which replica of yourself did you like best? The first or the second? If the answer is the first, apply for early retirement. If the answer is the second, resolve that from now on you'll reserve part of your mind for sitting out there with your audience, giving you sensible directions.

I hope you've discovered that the audience wants such pauses, mostly because it needs time to absorb all the verbal and visual information. Give them wall-to-wall words and they will switch your voice off!

It might take a while to overcome your natural compulsion to fill any silence with words and to experience silence as an embarrassing hiatus. Practise getting your pauses the right length and accepting their effect on your delivery.

What to do

Read aloud each of the following lines to a friend who can pretend to be an audience. Read each without, then with, the pause. When you put in the pause, make it at least two heart beats long and while it runs, look from one place in your imaginary audience to another.

'If we can't cure our own dependence on drugs ... [*pause*] ... then when our children get hooked ... [*pause*] ... we have no-one to blame but ourselves.'

'Get this, lads ... [*pause*] ... Ignore this one simple precaution ... [*pause*] ... and you'll find yourself at 10 000 feet in an expensive machine with the flying qualities of a wheelbarrow.'

'You've been told that the government recognises your equality ... [*pause*] ... you've been told that the law guarantees your equality ... [*pause*] ... you have even been told ... [*pause*] ... hah! ... that you now have equality ... [*pause*] ... but you and I know that if you want to be equal to men at the highest levels of business you have to be better than equal!'

Feel the difference? Feel the power of the pause? Remember to act it, don't just say it.

Once a question or interjection leaves someone's lips, the whole audience owns it. Even if most of them disagree with what has been said. This is why you need to make a special effort to avoid locking on to the questioner throughout your response. Practise sharing your reply with the whole audience.

What to do

Persuade at least four friends or colleagues to be an audience for two minutes. Tell them what you're doing. Explain that you want someone to interrupt with a question about half a minute or less after you start speaking. (Ask them not to make it a nasty question, just an ordinary open-ended 'how' or 'why' question.)

On the first run, deliberately do NOT share the reply — direct it to the questioner and no-one else.

Now ask the questioner to interrupt again with the same question. This time share the reply as described above.

Ask

- What was the difference?
- Which way did you feel you had more control?
- Ask your audience which one they preferred.

Perhaps you've been running small groups and meetings for years, never done this and never felt the need. I can only say fly it and feel the difference!

Most of us have an insistent voice in our heads that can talk us into failure when we are speaking in public. Being stuck in your own head listening to everything that can go wrong means there's no-one at the helm — looking out for the audience's interests!

You need to get out of your own head and into theirs — and once you do, that destructive inner voice falls silent and you start to win the empathy of the audience.

But you will always have to consciously correct and alter your self-talk. Especially if the unexpected happens and you come under pressure. Knowing what to tell yourself directs your physical and emotional responses and keeps you in control and focused on your purpose with the audience.

What to do
Think back on your last couple of presentations. In the left-hand column jot down interjections from the audience or sticky situations that might have, or did, start you on the road to destructive self-talk. Fill in the other two columns accordingly.

REMARK/SITUATION	NEGATIVE SELF-TALK	POSITIVE SELF-TALK

When we try to change our beliefs and attitudes it is important to explore our gut-level responses to new ideas. After all, beliefs aren't changed at the conscious thinking level; they're changed at the feeling level. Achieving flow will be your biggest step towards speaking comfortably and well in public — and enjoying it.

What to do

For your next three presentations keep a record of your gut-level responses to using the four keys to flow suggested in Chapter 2. Go over your visceral responses to using these keys and consider trialling a different key or rewording a key that seems to be working well.

The 'flow' meter

	MY RESPONSE TO				WHAT MIGHT
	LETTING GO OF THE BUSH	GETTING OUT OF MY HEAD	TALKING TO REAL PEOPLE	PASSING THE PASSION TEST	WORK BETTER FOR *ME*
PRESENTATION 1 Date:					
PRESENTATION 2 Date:					
PRESENTATION 3 Date:					
PRESENTATION 4 Date:					

activity 15 energy level check

The energy we put into addressing people is crucial for keeping the audience invested and awake. Our energy level is made up of eight components: speed, tone, pitch, volume, intensity, body language, emphasis and silence.

What to do

When you next find yourself in an audience — even if you're watching a speaker on television — try to identify these elements of energy and see if the speaker is using all or most of them to increase their impact on the audience. For example, think about whether the speaker is using the full tonal range of their voice, whether they vary the pace of their speech and whether their body language shows keenness and enthusiasm. Note your observations in the table below. This will bring home to you how much is won or lost in the energy stakes.

Try this

Have an honest friend who has seen you speak in public fill in one of these about you.

	WAS THIS ELEMENT DETECTABLE?	WAS IMPACT MAXIMISED?	OVERALL EFFECT?
SPEED			
TONE			
PITCH			
VOLUME			
INTENSITY			
BODY LANGUAGE			
EMPHASIS			
SILENCE			

activity 16 — *prepare with them in mind*

Are you asking the right kinds of questions about your audience before you prepare and structure your presentations? Facts might be facts, but there are as many ways to put them as there are audiences.

What to do

Run through this activity every time you are due to speak in public. Your whole approach to the presentation will be affected by the answers:

ABOUT THE AUDIENCE	

1. What kind of people will be there?
    Gender?
    Professions?
    Interests?	

2. Do they know each other?	

3. What do they know about the topic already?
    Are they up to date?
    Out of touch?
    Is there a mixture of expertise levels?	

4. Will there be anyone who knows more about the topic, or parts of it, than me?	

5. Why will they be there?
    Coerced?
    Because they want to be?
    A mix?	

6. What do they expect from you?	
ABOUT THE TOPIC	

7. How do the audience predominantly feel about the topic?
    Are they entrenched?
    Are they divided?
    What proportion feel one way, what proportion the other?
    How many are undecided?	

8. What's the worst question they're likely to ask?	

Delivery Form

On a blank sheet, create a city-view, brainstorm, link ideas, then transfer information onto this form

Audience ....

Date ....

Opening spotlight

City-view

Suburbs

Streets

....

....

....

....

....

....

....

....

....

....

Closing spotlight

'It's not what you tell them that counts. It's what they remember.'

MEDIA ASSOCIATES
TRAINING PEOPLE FOR BUSINESS

Prepare each presentation you do in this order:

1. Write the city-view
Use the city-view generator to write your bottom-line purpose with the audience.

2. Brainstorm and research
Brainstorm first, then add more with normal factual research.

3. Connect your ideas
Connect ideas using coloured pens.

4. Organise your ideas
Transfer ideas onto the Delivery Form. Give each column a suburb heading. Add opening and closing spotlights.

Deliver your presentation from the Delivery Form in this order:

	LONGER FORMAL SPEECHES	SHORTER INFORMAL SPEECHES
INTRODUCTION	opening spotlight city-view suburbs preview duration and questions?	opening spotlight city-view
MAIN BODY	suburb and streets suburb and streets suburb and streets	streets
CONCLUSION	suburbs review city-view review closing spotlight	city-view review closing spotlight

1. Check the layout of the room.
   Are the tables and chairs arranged as you want them? ☐
   Will everyone be able to see you? ☐
   Will you be able to see everyone? ☐
2. Check every detail down to coloured pens (are all your
   notes, slides, etc., present and in sequence?). ☐
3. Is the promised equipment there? ☐
4. Are all the visual aids in place? ☐
5. Are the visual aids in the best location? ☐
6. Will the audience be comfortable? ☐
   Does the air conditioning need turning up or down? ☐
   Will they have light shining directly in their eyes? ☐
7. Does everything work and can you work everything? ☐
   Make sure all technical equipment is ready to go. ☐
   Make sure you know which buttons to press. ☐
8. If you're dependent on someone else to cue the computer
   display, or slide change, go over the cues with that person. ☐
9. If you have sound effects, make sure the volume is set at the
   right level. ☐
10. For large venues, check the lighting to be directed at you.
    Best is two lights, 45 degrees to each side of centre and
    45 degrees up from horizontal. ☐
11. Is the lectern too high or too low? If it's above your sternum
    it's too high. ☐
12. Can the microphone be moved from the lectern? If it can,
    find out how. If it can't, choose between staying behind the
    lectern and forgetting both lectern and microphone. ☐
13. Check how to speak into the microphone. Each microphone
    type has its own personality. Make sure you can still be heard if
    you turn your head. ☐
14. Is the microphone at the right sound level? Check with the
    technician. ☐
15. Make sure the person introducing you will be doing so
    appropriately. ☐

■ SELECTED QUOTABLE QUOTES

'Next to being witty yourself, the best thing is being able to quote another's wit.'
Christian N. Bovee

This selection is very personal, with quotes that move me or make me laugh. Perhaps you'll find a few here that give you the same responses. My apologies to the prolific genius with the pseudonym *Anon* or *Unkown*.

achievement
'Give me a standing place and I will move the world.' *Archimedes*

'The rooster makes more racket than the hen that lays the egg.' *Joel Harri*

'We can't all be heroes because someone has to sit on the curb and clap as they go by.' *Will Rogers*

adversity
'Adversity has the effect of eliciting talents which in prosperous circumstances would have lain dormant.' *Horace*

'I'll say this for adversity: people seem to be able to stand it, and that's more than I can say for prosperity.' *Kin Hubbard*

advertising
'Advertising may be described as the science of arresting the human intelligence long enough to get money from it.' *Stephen Leacock*

advice
'"Be yourself" is about the worst advice you can give some people.' *Tom Masson*

age and youth
'When your friends begin to flatter you on how young you look, it's a sure sign you're getting old.' *Mark Twain*

'Youth is wasted on the young.' *George Bernard Shaw*

'Except for the occasional heart attack, I feel as young as I ever did.' *Robert Benchley*

'First you forget names, then you forget faces, then you forget to pull your zipper up, then you forget to pull it down.' *Leo Rosenburg*

ambition
'Most people would succeed in small things if they were not troubled by great ambitions.' *Longfellow*

anger

'Never get angry. Never make a threat. Reason with people.' *Don Corleone, The Godfather*

belief

'He who is firm and resolute in will moulds the world to himself.' *Goethe*

'The most unhappy of all men is he who believes himself to be so.' *Hume*

the Bible

'I've read the last page of the Bible. It's going to turn out all right.' *Billy Graham*

business

'Everything comes to him who hustles while he waits.' *Thomas A. Edison*

'Promise bronze, deliver gold.' *Media Associates*

change

'Things do not change. We change.' *Henry Thoreau*

character

'Smooth runs the water where the brook is deep.' *Shakespeare*

'To reform a man you must begin with his grandmother.' *Victor Hugo*

children

'Your children are not your children. They are the sons and daughters of Life's longing for itself.' *Kahlil Gibran*

'A child can ask a thousand questions that the wisest man cannot answer.' *J. Abbott*

'If I could get to the highest place in Athens, I would lift up my voice and say, "What mean you, fellow citizens, that ye turn every stone to scrape wealth together, and take so little care of your children to whom ye must one day relinquish all?"' *Socrates*

church

'Most of us spend the first six days of each week sowing wild oats, then we go to church on Sunday and pray for a crop failure.' *Fred Allen*

communication

'Men of few words are the best men.' *Shakespeare*

compassion

'We have all sufficient strength to endure the misfortunes of others.' *La Rochefoucauld*

conceit

'An egotist is a man who talks so much about himself that he gives me no time to talk about myself.' *H.L. Wayland*

'He was like a cock who thought the sun had risen to hear him crow.' *George Eliot*

condemnation

'They condemn what they do not understand.' *Cicero*

conferences

'No grand idea was ever born in a conference, but a lot of foolish ideas have died there.' *F. Scott Fitzgerald*

connections

'All things are connected.' *Chief Seattle*

'I am a part of all that I have met.' *Tennyson*

conscience

'A man who had his wallet stolen received some of it back, with a letter. "Sur, sum years ago I stole your muny. Remorse is gnawin' me, so I send sum back. When it gnaws me again I will send sum more."' *Public Speaker's Treasure Chest*

conversation

'He has occasional flashes of silence that make his conversation perfectly delightful.' *Sydney Smith*

'At the bottom of a good deal of bravery that appears in the world there lurks a miserable cowardice. Men will face powder and steel because they cannot face public opinion.' *E.H.Chapin*

criticism

'If we had no failings ourselves, we should not take so much pleasure in finding out about those of others.' *La Rochefoucauld*

'Critics are like eunuchs in a harem: they know how it's done, they've seen it done every day, but they're unable to do it themselves.' *Brendan Behan*

death

'Cowards die many times before their deaths; the valiant never taste of death but once.' *Shakespeare*

'When death, the great reconciler, has come, it is never our tenderness that we repent of, but our severity.' *George Eliot*

'Why fear death? It is the most beautiful adventure in life'. *Charles Frohman*

'I'm not afraid to die, I just don't want to be there when it happens.' *Woody Allen*

defeat

'What is defeat? Nothing but education, nothing but the first step to something better.' *Wendell Phillips*

democracy

'Elections are held to delude the populace into believing that they are participating in government.' *Gerald F. Lieberman*

'We go by the major vote, and if the majority are insane, the sane must go to hospital.' *H. Mann*

desire

'Ours is a world where people don't know what they want and are willing to go through hell to get it.' *Don Marquis*

'There are two tragedies in life. One is not to get your heart's desire. The other is to get it.' *George Bernard Shaw*

destruction

'Whom the gods wish to destroy they first call promising.' *Cyril Connolly*

determination

'Either I will find a way, or I will make one.' *Sir Philip Sidney*

'If at first you don't succeed, try, try again. Then quit. There's no use being a damn fool about it.' *W.C. Fields*

'The best lightning-rod for your protection is your own spine.' *Emerson*

diets

'I went on a diet, swore off drinking and heavy eating, and in 14 days I lost two weeks.' *Joe Lewis*

differences

'It is always the minorities that hold the key of progress; it is always through those who are unafraid to be different that advance comes to human society.' *Raymond B. Fosdick*

difficult

'Why be difficult when with a little effort you could be impossible.' *Unknown*

diplomacy

'The art of saying "nice doggy" while you look for a stick.' *Unknown*

disapproval

Lady Astor: 'Mr Churchill, you're disgusting. If you were my husband, I'd poison your coffee.' *Churchill*: 'Madam, if you were my wife, I'd drink it.'

discontent

'Discontent is the first step in the progress of a man or a nation.' *Oscar Wilde*

dogs

'We had to have the dog put down for worrying sheep. It used to slink up to them and whisper, "Mint sauce".' *Public Speaker's Treasure Chest*

drink

'I always keep a supply of stimulant handy in case I see a snake — which I also keep handy.' *W.C. Fields*

'I distrust camels and anyone else who can go a week without a drink.' *Joe Lewis*

Lady Astor: 'Mr Churchill, you're drunk.' *Churchill*: 'Yes, madam, but you're ugly and in the morning I'll be sober.'

'Work is the curse of the drinking class.' *Oscar Wilde*

economists

'If all economists were laid end to end, they would not reach a conclusion.' *George Bernard Shaw*

education

'A mixture of misery and education is highly explosive.' *Herbert Samuel*

'Teaching is the fine art of imparting knowledge without possessing it.' *Mark Twain*

effectiveness

'Efficiency is doing things right. Effectiveness is doing the right things.' *Peter Drucker*

enemies

'Always forgive your enemies. Nothing annoys them so much.' *Oscar Wilde*

'He makes no friend who never made a foe.' *Tennyson*

'The greatest happiness is to vanquish your enemies, to chase them before you, to rob them of their wealth, to see those dear to them bathed in tears, to clasp to your bosom their wives and daughters.' *Genghis Khan*

environment

'When the insects take over the world we hope they will remember, with gratitude, how we took them along on all our picnics.' *Bill Vaughn*

failure

'What would you attempt to do if you knew you couldn't fail?' *Robert Schiller*

family

'It is a wise father that knows his own child.' *Shakespeare*

'He's a good boy. Everything he steals he brings right home to his mother.' *Fred Allen*

'Parents are the last people on earth who ought to have children.' *Samuel Butler*

'Parents were invented to make children happy by giving them something to ignore.' *Ogden Nash*

'People who say they sleep like a baby usually don't have one.' *Leo J. Burke*

'The first half of our life is ruined by our parents and the second half by our children.' *Clarence Darrow*

'We learn from experience. A man never wakes up his second baby just to see it smile.' *Grace Williams*

famous last words

'Heavier-than-air flying machines are impossible.' *Lord Kelvin, President, Royal Society, 1895*

'Everything that can be invented has been invented.' *Charles Duell, commissioner U.S. Office of Patents, 1899*

'This "telephone" has too many shortcomings to be seriously considered as a means of communication. The device is inherently of no value to us.' *Western Union internal memo, 1876*

'I think there is a world market for maybe five computers.' *Thomas Watson, Chairman, IBM, 1943*

'Airplanes are interesting toys but of no military value.' *Marshal Foch, Professor of Strategy, School of War*

fashion
'Fashion is a form of ugliness so intolerable it has to be altered every six months.' *Unknown*

faults
'Men do not suspect faults which they do not commit.' *Samuel Johnson*

forgiveness
'To forgive is to set a prisoner free, and to know that the prisoner was me.' *Anon*

fortune
'Fortune is not on the side of the faint-hearted.' *Sophocles*

freedom
'Liberty means responsibility. That is why most men dread it.' *George Bernard Shaw*

generosity
'How much easier it is to be generous than just! Men are sometimes bountiful who are not honest.' *Junius*

genius

'There is no great genius without tincture of madness.' *Seneca*

giving and receiving

'He who waits to do a great deal of good at once, will never do anything.' *Samuel Johnson*

'And there are those who give and know not pain in giving, nor do they seek joy, nor give with mindfulness of virtue; They give as in yonder valley the myrtle breathes its fragrance into space.' *Kahlil Gibran*

'Rich gifts wax poor when givers prove unkind.' *Shakespeare*

God

'I sometimes think that God in creating man somewhat over-estimated His ability.' *Oscar Wilde*

'God will forgive me; that's His business.' *Public Speaker's Treasure Chest*

'If only God would give me some clear sign! Like making a large deposit in my name at a Swiss bank.' *Woody Allen*

good and bad

'There is nothing either good or bad, but thinking makes it so.' *Shakespeare*

'Of the good in you I can speak, but not of the evil. For what is evil but good tortured by its own hunger and thirst.' *Kahlil Gibran*

government

'The best government is a benevolent tyranny tempered by an occasional assassination.' *Voltaire*

'There's no trick to being a humorist when you have the whole government working for you.' *Will Rogers*

health

'The art of medicine consists of amusing the patient while nature cures the disease.' *Voltaire*

honesty

'Make yourself an honest man, and then you may be sure that there is one rascal less in the world.' *Carlyle*

honour

'The louder he talked of his honour, the faster we counted our spoons.' *Ralph Waldo Emerson*

'When faith is lost and honour dies, the man is dead.' *John G. Whittier*

humanity

'Humanity is the Son of God.' *Theodore Parker*

'There is but one race — humanity.' *George Moore*

idealist

'An idealist is a man with both feet planted firmly in the air.' *Franklin D. Roosevelt*

ideas

'It is only liquid currents of thought that move men and the world.' *Wendel Phillips*

'No army can withstand the strength of an idea whose time has come.' *Victor Hugo*

imagination

'Every great advance in science has issued from a new audacity of imagination.'
John Dewey

immortality

'Millions long for immortality who do not know what to do with themselves on a rainy
Sunday afternoon.' *Susan Ertz*

inheritance

'The meek shall inherit the earth ... but not the mineral rights.' *J. Paul Getty*

intellectuals

'An intellectual is a person educated beyond his intelligence.' *Brandon Matthews*

'An intellectual is a man who takes more words than necessary to tell more than he
knows.' *Dwight D. Eisenhower*

journalists

'One of the greatest of destructive forces is the journalist who believes the whole world
to be either corrupt or incompetent and that it only remains to dig out the evidence.'
Media Associates

joy and sorrow

'Everyone can master a grief but he that has it.' *Shakespeare*

'He who has so little knowledge of human nature as to seek happiness by changing
anything but his own disposition, will waste his life in fruitless efforts, and multiply the
griefs which he purposes to remove.' *Johnson*

'The deeper the sorrow the less tongue it hath.' *Talmud*

'The deeper that sorrow carves into your being, the more joy you can contain. Is not the
cup that holds your wine the very cup that was burned in the potter's oven? And is not
the lute that soothes your spirit the very wood that was hollowed with knives?'

Kahlil Gibran

justice

'If England treats her criminals the way she has treated me, she doesn't deserve to have any.' *Oscar Wilde*

'Ignorance of the law excuses no man from practising it.' *Addison Mizner*

'The efficiency of our criminal jury system is only marred by the difficulty of finding 12 men every day who don't know anything and can't read.' *Mark Twain*

knowledge and ignorance

'There is only one good, namely, knowledge; and only one evil, namely, ignorance.' *Socrates*

'Give a man a fish and you feed him for a day. Teach him how to fish and you feed him for a lifetime.' *Confucius*

'No man can be a pure specialist without being in the strict sense an idiot.' *George Bernard Shaw*

'To be proud of learning is the greatest ignorance.' *Jeremy Taylor*

'Who are a little wise, the best fools be.' *John Donne*

laws

'Laws are spider webs through which the big flies pass and the little ones get caught'. *Honoré de Balzac*

life and society

'Early to bed and early to rise is a bad rule for anyone who wishes to become acquainted with our most prominent and influential people.' *George Ade*

'Anybody who goes to see a psychiatrist ought to have his head examined.' *Samuel Goldwyn*

'It's useless to hold a person to any anything he says while he's in love, drunk, or running for office.' *Shirley MacLaine*

'Never keep up with the Joneses. Drag them down to your level. It's cheaper.' *Quentin Crisp*

'There's nothing so nice as doing good by stealth and being found out by accident.' *Charles Lamb*

'May you live all the days of your life.' *Jonathon Swift*

'Don't take life so seriously. You're not going to get out alive anyway.' *Unknown*

'There is more to life than increasing its speed.' *Mahatma Ghandi*

'It matters not how long you live, but how well.' *Publius Syrius*

light

'Due to technical difficulties the light at the end of the tunnel has been switched off.' *Unknown*

listening

'Know how to listen and you will profit even from those who talk badly.' *Plutarch*

loyalty

'It goes far toward making a man faithful to let him understand that you think him so; and he that does but suspect I will deceive him, gives me a sort of right to do it.' *Seneca*

love

'No man at one time can be wise and love.' *Robert Herrick*

'Tis better to have loved and lost than never to have loved at all.' *Tennyson*

'He gave her a look you could have poured on a waffle.' *Rilg Lardner*

'Love doesn't make the world go round. Love is what makes the ride worthwhile.' *Franklin P. Jones*

'Never go to bed mad. Stay up and fight.' *Phyllis Diller*

'To love oneself is the beginning of a life-long romance.' *Oscar Wilde*

mañana

'Never put off till tomorrow what you can do the day after tomorrow.' *Mark Twain*

marriage

'Sing and dance together and be joyous, but let each one of you be alone, even as the strings of a lute are alone though they quiver with the same music.' *Kahlil Gibran*

'I have a parrot that swears, a stove that smokes and a cat that stays out at night. What would I want with a husband.' *Old Yankee spinster*

media

'Freedom of the press is limited to those who own one.' *A.J. Liebling*

'Newspaper editors are men who separate the wheat from the chaff, then print the chaff.' *Adlai Stevenson*

middle of the road

'We know what happens to people who stay in the middle of the road. They get run over.' *Aneurin Bevan*

misers

'Misers aren't fun to live with, but they make wonderful ancestors.' *Dave Brenner*

mistakes

'A man who makes no mistakes does not usually make anything.' *Edward J. Phelps*

mob

'It is the proof of a bad cause when it is applauded by the mob.' *Seneca*

motivation

'Every production of genius must be the production of enthusiasm.' *Benjamin Disraeli*

'A nation is a society united by a delusion about its ancestry and by a common hatred of its neighbours.' *Dean William R. Inge*

nature

'Nature is the living, visible garment of God.' *Goethe*

'Nature is the most thrifty thing in the world; she undergoes change, but there's no annihilation — the essence remains.' *T. Binney*

noble

'It is more noble to give yourself completely to one individual than to labour diligently for the salvation of the masses.' *Dag Hammarskjold*

nonsense

'No one is exempt from talking nonsense; the misfortune is to do it solemnly.' *Montaigne*

nothingness

'Of all the immensities around us in the world, the greatest of these is nothingness.' *Leonardo da Vinci*

pain

'Much of your pain is self-chosen. It is the bitter potion by which the physician within you heals your sick self.' *Kahlil Gibran*

patriotism

'A real patriot is the fellow who gets a parking ticket and rejoices that the system works.' *Bill Vaughn*

'Patriotism is the last refuge of a scoundrel.' *Samuel Johnson*

people

'People are not born bastards, they have to work at it.' *Frank Dane*

personal abuse

'He had the sort of face that always wants to see the manager.' *Public Speaker's Treasure Chest*

'I refuse to have a battle of wits with an unarmed person.' *Unknown*

'I am not a complete idiot. Some parts are missing.' *Unknown*

'He used to think he was indecisive, but now he's not so sure.' *Public Speaker's Treasure Chest*

'Amazing to think that you beat out 50 million other sperm.' *Unknown*

'I'm afraid [person] can't be here today. It was a full moon last night.' *Public Speaker's Treasure Chest*

'This man is depriving a village somewhere of an idiot.' *Unknown*

'Since he started to wear a pace-maker, every time he makes love his garage door opens.' *Public Speaker's Treasure Chest*

'She's descended from a long line her mother listened to.' *Gypsy Rose Lee*

politics
'A government that robs Peter to pay Paul can always depend on the support of Paul.' *George Bernard Shaw*

'He knows nothing and thinks he knows everything. That points clearly to a political career.' *George Bernard Shaw*

posterity
'I would much rather that posterity should inquire why no statues were erected to me, than why they were.' *Cato*

power
'Nothing in the world is more haughty than a man of moderate capacity when once raised to power.' *Wessenburg*

'The mightiest powers by deepest calms are fed.' *B.W. Procter*

prejudice
'Prejudice is the child of ignorance.' *William Hazlitt*

principles
'There comes a time to put aside principles and do what's right.' *Public Speaker's Treasure Chest*

'When a man says he approves of something in principle, it means he hasn't the slightest intention of putting it into practice.' *Prince Otto von Bismark*

public speaking
'Instruments have been invented that will throw a speaker's voice more than a mile. Now we need an instrument that will throw the speaker an equal distance.' *Public Speaker's Treasure Chest*

'I've seen a lot of guys who are smarter than I am and a lot who know more about cars. And yet I've lost them in the smoke. Why? Because I'm tough? No … You've got to know how to talk to them, plain and simple.' *Lee Iacocca*

'Some after dinner speakers are not only loquacious, but they also talk too much.' *Toastmasters Treasure Chest*

'You have noticed that the less I know about a subject, the more confidence I have; and the more light I throw on it.' *Mark Twain*

'[After a mistake] I'd commit suicide, but then what would I do for an encore.' *Toastmasters Treasure Chest*

purpose
'If you don't know where you're going, any road will take you there.' *Koran*

religion
'Religion is excellent stuff for keeping common people quiet.' *Napoleon Bonaparte*

respect
'Jesus may love you but will he respect you in the morning?' *Unknown*

reward
'He who wishes to secure the good of others has already secured his own.' *Confucius*

sex
'Children should never discuss sex in the presence of their elders.' *Gregory Nunn*

'It has to be admitted that we English have sex on the brain, which is a very unfortunate place to have it.' *Malcolm Muggeridge*

'Of all sexual aberrations, chastity is the strangest.' *Anatole France*

'Of the delights of this world, man cares most for sexual intercourse, yet he has left it out of his heaven.' *Mark Twain*

'Confucius say: boy who go to bed with sex problem often wake with solution in hand.' *Unknown*

'Sexual intercourse is a grossly overrated pastime; the position is undignified, the pleasure momentary and the consequences utterly damnable.' *Lord Chesterfield*

sexual harassment
'Is sexual harassment at work a problem for the self-employed?' *Unknown*

sexual rivalry
'A woman without a man is like a fish without a bicycle.' *Gloria Steinem*

'I don't like her. But don't misunderstand me: my dislike is purely platonic.' *Sir Herbert Beerbohm Tree*

'If you think women are the weaker sex, try pulling sheets back to your side.'
Toastmasters Treasure Chest

'No-one should have to dance backward all their lives.' *Jill Ruckelshaus*

sincerity

'A little sincerity is a dangerous thing, and a great deal of it is absolutely fatal.'
Oscar Wilde

speech and silence

'Blessed is the man who, having nothing to say, abstains from giving in words evidence of the fact.' *George Eliot*

'For thought is a bird of space, that in a cage of words may indeed unfold its wings but cannot fly.' *Kahlil Gibran*

'Speech is a faculty given to man to conceal his thoughts.' *Talleyrand*

spirituality

'We are not human beings having a spiritual experience. We are spiritual beings having a human experience.' *Teilhard de Chardin*

statistics

'Statistics are like a bikini. What they reveal is suggestive, but what they conceal is vital.' *Aaron Levenstein*

success

'Success is not a matter of spontaneous combustion. You have to set yourself alight.'
Abraham Lincoln

surrealism

'How many surrealists does it take to screw in a light bulb? Two: one to hold the giraffe and the other to fill the bathtub with machine tools.' *Unknown*

tact

'Tact is the ability to describe others as they see themselves.' *Abraham Lincoln*

tears

'Tears are the noble language of the eye.' *Robert Herrick*

television

'I find television very educating. Every time somebody turns on the set I go into the other room and read a book.' *Groucho Marx*

temptation

'No man is matriculated to the art of life till he has been well tempted.' *George Eliot*

toilet

'Confucius say: man who stand on toilet is high on pot.' *Unknown*

truth & lies

'And if you would know God, be not therefore a solver of riddles. Rather look about you and you shall see Him playing with your children.' *Kahlil Gibran*

'A thing is not necessarily true because a man dies for it.' *Oscar Wilde*

virginity

'Virginity is like a balloon. One prick and it's gone.' *Unknown*

wealth

'I'm living so far beyond my income that we may almost be said to be living apart.' *e e cummings*

'If you want to get rich from writing, write the sort of thing that's read by persons who move their lips when they're reading to themselves.' *Don Marquis*

wisdom

'That which seems the height of absurdity in one generation often becomes the height of wisdom in another.' *Adlai Stevenson*

wit

'Brevity is the soul of wit.' *Shakespeare*

'Wit is a sword; it is meant to make people feel the point as well as see it.' *G.K.Chesterton*

work

'Work is the refuge of people who have nothing better to do.' *Oscar Wilde*

BIBLIOGRAPHY

Cohen, Herb 1997, *You Can Negotiate Anything*, Herb Cohen

Covey, Stephen R. 1993, *Seven Habits of Highly Effective People*, The Business Library, Melbourne

Damasio, Antonio 1996, *Descartes' Error*, Papermac, London

Goleman, Daniel, *Emotional Intelligence*, Bloomsbury, London

Gray, Malcolm 1991, *Public Speaking*, Schwartz and Wilkinson, Melbourne

Humes, James C. 1991, *The Language of Leadership*, The Business Library, Melbourne

Mehrabian, Albert and Ferris, Susan 1967, 'Inference of attitudes from non-verbal communication in two channels', *Journal of Consulting Psychology*, vol. 31, no. 3, pp. 248–52

Toogood, Granville N. 1995, *The Articulate Executive*, McGraw-Hill, Sydney

Mehrabian, Albert and Weiner, Moreton 1967, 'Decoding of inconsistent communications', *Journal of Personality and Social Psychology*, vol. 6, no. 1, pp. 100–14.

INDEX